VANOISE SKI TOURING

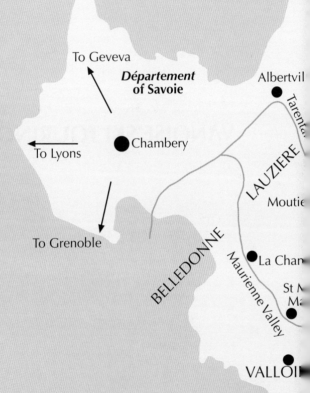

THE VANOISE AND SURROUNDING AREA

Aiguille des Glaciers
3816m

ITALY

BEAUFORTAIN   Bourg St. Maurice

River Isère   Mont
Pourri
3779m

Aiguille de la Grande
Sassière
3747m

Grande Casse
3852m

GLACIERS
DE LA
VANOISE

VAL D'ISERE

CARRO / EVETTES

Bonneval

River Arc

AVEROLE

nel de
enne

Modane

AMBIN VALLEY

MONT
THABOR

ITALY

ABOUT THE AUTHOR

Paul Henderson was born in Durham in 1963. His love for the
mountains started at school with walks in the Lake District, but his
main interest quickly turned to rock-climbing. He was first introduced to skiing on family holidays to the Lecht in the Cairngorms
long before the lifts were installed. His skiing career really began
with ski trips to the Alps in the late 1980s. On moving to France, in
1995, he was introduced to the delights of ski touring by French
friends and soon became obsessed by this new sport. He has spent
the last seven years exploring the mountains around his new home
on foot as well as on skis. The idea for this guide was born when he
realised friends that had spent their whole lives in the area were
asking for advice about where to go.

He lives in Chambéry with his wife Alice, where he works as an
English teacher and translator.

VANOISE SKI TOURING

by
Paul Henderson

2 POLICE SQUARE, MILNTHORPE, CUMBRIA LA7 7PY
www.cicerone.co.uk

© Paul Henderson 2002
ISBN 1 85284 375 6
A catalogue record for this book is available from the British Library

ACKNOWLEDGEMENTS
I would like to thank my wife, Alice, for all her encouragement and for being prepared to go skiing with me even when the conditions were awful!

A special mention must go to a great friend, Richard Champeney, for his enthusiasm and support, and to his wife, Jo, for allowing him to spend so many of his holidays in the mountains with me.

I would also like to thank my friends, Claude and Marie-Christine Bertholet, Pierre Lortet and Philippe and Jeanne Roche, for showing me the ropes at the beginning of my ski touring career, and for being willing partners on some of my more exploratory outings.

Finally, thanks must also go to Philip Whitick for his constructive criticism and help in correcting the text.

Advice to Readers

Readers are advised that while every effort is taken by the author to ensure the accuracy of this guidebook, changes can occur which may affect the contents. It is advisable to check locally on transport, accommodation, shops, etc, but even rights of way can be altered.

The publisher would welcome notes of any such changes.

WARNING

Mountaineering can be a dangerous activity carrying a risk of personal injury or death. It should be undertaken only by those with a full understanding of the risks and with the training and experience to evaluate them. Mountaineers should be appropriately equipped for the routes undertaken. Whilst every care and effort has been taken in the preparation of this guide, the user should be aware that conditions, especially in winter, can be highly variable and can change quickly. Holds may become loose or fall off, rockfall can affect the character of a route, snow and avalanche conditions must be carefully considered. These can materially affect the seriousness of a climb, tour or expedition.

Therefore, except for any liability which cannot be excluded by law, neither Cicerone nor the author accepts liability for damage of any nature (including damage to property, personal injury or death) arising directly or indirectly from the information in this guide.

Cover photograph: Traversing the Col de Comberousse to the Col de la Valloire on Day 2 of the Belledonne tour (photo by Sebastien Perrier)

CONTENTS

On the Glacier de Gébroulaz, below the Dôme de Polset on Day 5 of the Glaciers de la Vanoise tour

INTRODUCTION

There is no denying that the mountains of Savoie are spectacularly beautiful. The proud pyramids of the Aiguilles d'Arves, the austere northface of the Grande Casse and the sparkling 'Dômes' of the Vanoise Glaciers are as fine examples of mountain architecture as can be found anywhere. But there is more to the area than a collection of points of outstanding natural beauty. The geographical diversity of the region is a reflection of the different facets of Savoie's complex personality: from the savageness of the Belledonne to the gentleness of the Beaufortain, from the ostentation of the Aiguille d'Arves to the aloofness of the Haute Maurienne. The tours described in this guide reflect the variety of landscape and skiing that makes ski touring in Savoie so special. The area is however best known to skiers for the Olympic ski-resorts of Tignes, Val d'Isère, Les Arcs, La Plagne and The Three Valleys, which lie on the northern edge of the Vanoise National Park.

The Vanoise National Park, situated in the *département* of Savoie, was the first national park to be created in France. As the park has been protected from the encroachment of the ski-resorts, it has been preserved as one of the great ski-touring areas of the French Alps.

The richness of the area for ski touring also lies in Savoie's lesser-known massifs, such as the Lauzière, the Belledonne, the Beaufortain and the Haute Maurienne, which surround the Vanoise. This guide provides an introduction to all the different parts of this region and corresponds, more or less, to the French *département* of Savoie (with minor incursions into the neighbouring *départements* of Isère and Les Hautes Alpes) giving an overview of the wonderful and varied ski touring to be had here.

Vanoise Ski Touring is aimed at both experienced ski tourers and mountaineers who would like to get away from the hurly-burly of the ski-resorts. Ski touring is about much more than skiing ability; mountain skills such as navigation, glacier travel and avalanche awareness are indispensable. The safest way to start ski touring is with a mountain guide, this being especially true for skiers with no previous mountaineering experience.

Many of the tours start from resorts, though tours that are basically off-piste trails are not included; good off-piste skiing guides already exist for many of the major resorts. The guide should, however, be useful for people who would like to tour for just one or two days as part of a resort holiday.

The organisation of the guide follows the natural division of the Savoie

The final slopes below the Pointe Francesetti on Day 5 of the Carro/Evettes tour

département into its various geographical areas. The various types of tours were selected, as far as possible, to reflect the atmosphere of these areas and to provide interesting and homogenous excursions. In general, preference has been given to multiday, hut-to-hut tours but in some areas it is more logical to do a number of day trips from a mountain hut or a base-camp in the valley. The tours involve up to six day's skiing, although most can be lengthened or shortened to suit time constraints, weather conditions and fitness.

Given good snow conditions, most of the tours are within the capabilities of any competent skier (ie. someone who is at ease on black slopes), but it must be remembered that snow conditions are not often

perfect when you are touring. A final chapter describes some classic tours that fall more into the realm of ski mountaineering than ski touring. None of the tours in the guide can be considered extreme skiing.

It must be remembered that ski touring is both a physically demanding and a potentially dangerous sport; it is important not to over-estimate your fitness or technical abilities. Skinning uphill, with four kilograms of ski, binding and boot on each foot and a 10–15kg rucksack on your back, is an exhausting business. Do not expect to be able to do a 1500m climb every day unless you are very fit.

Most serious accidents are caused by avalanches, although crevasses, seracs and steep slopes, especially if there are cliffs in the fall-line, can also be extremely dangerous. General mountaineering knowledge and experience is at least as valuable as skiing ability if you want to have a long and safe ski-touring career.

GEOGRAPHY

This guide covers the mountains south of Mont Blanc and north of the Ecrins Massif. The western part is defined by the Grésivaudan Valley, which runs from Chambéry to Grenoble, the eastern edge by the Franco-Italian border.

This area is divided into three sections by the valleys of the River Isère (the Tarentaise Valley) and the River Arc (the Maurienne Valley). The Vanoise National Park, which lies between these two valleys, contains most of the highest mountains. The largest ski-resorts are on the northern and western edges of the Vanoise and provide convenient access points to the area. The Beaufortain lies to the north of the Vanoise, the Lauzière and Belledonne to the west and Valloire, Mont Thabor and the Haute Maurienne to the south.

ACCESS

To get to all of the locations described in this book, it is necessary to pass through Chambéry. Chambéry is about 80km south of Geneva and 100km east of Lyons. There are regular, cheap flights from the UK to both these airports as well as to Chambéry itself. There is a shuttle-bus service

On the summit ridge below the Levanna Occidentale on Day 2 of the Carro/Evettes tour

13

Skinning up the Col de Corne Noire on Day 2 in the Beaufortain with the Crête du Rey in the background

between Lyons airport and Chambéry and a train service from Geneva airport to Chambéry.

From Chambéry it is possible to get to most of the larger resorts using a combination of train and bus services. Unfortunately, public transport starts to become less reliable when the resorts close in the middle of April; the best time for touring in the higher areas is generally April to May. Contact the relevant tourist office for further details (see Appendix 2).

By far the easiest way to reach the start of most of the tours is by car. The road access from Chambéry is described at the start of each section.

SNOW CONDITIONS AND AVALANCHES

SNOW CONDITIONS

As in all mountain areas, the weather and therefore the snow conditions can be very variable. The snowpack can be very unstable in winter, especially in the higher areas (above 2500m). The best time for ski touring is March to May. If you want to go touring earlier in the season, it is best to stay in the lower massifs. All skiers dream of finding 50cm of virgin powder; that light, 'fluffy' snow that gives you the sensation that you are floating down the mountainside. Seasoned ski tourers know that spring snow, produced by the freeze-thaw action of the sun, can be equally sublime to ski. They delight in finding rock-hard névé, knowing that when the top few centimetres melt as the day warms-

up, they will have the perfect skiing surface. It is rare for powder to last long on south-facing slopes, even the middle of winter.

On the other hand, after two weeks of good weather, spring snow can be found sometimes as early as February. With an astute choice of itinerary you can usually find good snow. No one makes the perfect choice every time and, because many tours include slopes with different aspects, you will undoubtedly come across difficult snow conditions from time to time. In crusty or very heavy snow, survival skiing becomes the watchword: 'hop and hope' often being the best turning technique! When slopes are very icy it may even be best to descend in crampons.

AVALANCHES

In an average year, 100 people are killed by avalanches in the Alps and you must be aware of the dangers. Please see the table on Avalanche Safety Information on the next page.

Information on snow conditions and the avalanche risk can be obtained (in French) by telephoning 08 92 68 10 20. These bulletins are updated every day at 4pm. The information they give is extremely useful in planning a tour but conditions can still vary locally. A seven day weather forecast can be obtained by dialling 08 92 68 02 73. The forecast is updated three times a day, at 7.30am, 12 noon and 6pm.

AVALANCHE SAFETY INFORMATION

This book is not a guide to avalanche awareness but some general points must be borne in mind when deciding where, or even whether, to go.

1. It is difficult to assess the snow conditions in an area without good knowledge of the terrain and recent weather conditions. Telephone snow reports, hut wardens, local mountain guides and, if you are in a resort, the ski-patrol can all provide indispensable information.

2. Even after several days of good weather, certain slopes can still be very dangerous. Weak layers in the snow-pack can last a surprisingly long time.

3. Learn to read the signs that may indicate unstable accumulations of snow; for example cornices, ripple marks, snow dunes etc.

4. If you are uncertain about the stability of a slope and it is impossible to avoid crossing it, do so one at a time and only stop in 'safe' zones, such as behind large rocks or trees.

5. The first person to ski a slope will not always be the person who triggers an avalanche. Sometimes several skiers can pass before the slope avalanches.

6. All members of a group should carry an avalanche transceiver and know how to use it. Each skier must also have an avalanche probe, in order to pin-point the exact position of the victim, and a snow shovel, to dig them out. A person buried by an avalanche has a good chance of survival if they are found within twenty minutes, however, by the time outside help arrives they will probably be dead. Your ability to find and free an avalanche victim could save a life.

7. There is no such thing as zero risk. Each party must assess the risks involved at any particular moment and make a decision accordingly.

Nearing the Refuge du Carro on the first day of the Carro/Evettes tour

EMERGENCIES

Where necessary (ie. when the route is not obvious or where the logistics are complicated) details of the quickest ways to reach civilisation in the event of bad weather or an accident occuring have been given. Often these escape routes are quite long but they are the fastest ways to evacuate an accident victim or the best ways out in bad weather.

It must be remembered that mobile phone coverage, away from ski-resorts, is still not perfect. The emergency services can be contacted by dialling 18.

The mountains are much more hostile in winter than in summer and the rescue services, although they will do their best, may not be able to reach accident victims quickly. In one

famous case in 1998, four ski tourers were trapped by bad weather near the Col de la Vanoise. They survived the ten days it took the rescue services to find them because they were extremely well equipped. Having the right equipment, and knowing how to use it, is vitally important.

N.B. All decisions about where to go, or even whether to go at all, must be taken by the individuals concerned, taking into account the weather and snow conditions at the time.

EQUIPMENT

It is possible to buy touring adaptors for standard downhill bindings but, for all but the shortest of tours, it is worth considering having special touring skis, boots and bindings. The

17

gains in weight and comfort during the climb more than compensate for the loss of performance during the descent.

A full set of touring gear is a big investment but it is possible to rent touring gear in many of the larger towns and resorts. A week's rental for touring skis, skins, boots, poles, avalanche transceiver, snow shovel and avalanche probe cost around 150€ to 200€ in 2002. As ski touring is growing in popularity, more and more outdoor shops have gear to rent: the local tourist office (see Appendix 2) should be able to give details of where you can rent ski touring gear (*matériel de ski de randonnée* in French).

Telemark skiers do not have to invest so heavily; all they need to add to standard telemark gear is a set of skins and *couteaux/harscheisen*.

It is often a good idea to carry a pair of crampons; the rock-hard *névé* that you climb in the morning can turn into perfect spring snow by lunchtime. When touring in the high mountains you should also take standard glacier gear (ie. ice-axe, rope, harness, one or two ice-screws, slings and prussick loops or jumars).

Avalanche transceivers are not an unnecessary luxury. These small devices, when correctly used, allow an avalanche victim to be found very quickly. Each member of the party should have one and know how to use it. They should be turned on and tested at the beginning of each day, even if the snow-pack seems perfectly stable. The day you decide to leave it at home is the day you will be

Approaching the summit of Mont Bellacha on the second day of the Lauzière tour

Leaving the Refuge du Fond d'Assois on Day 4 of the Glaceirs de la Vanoise tour

caught by a very unexpected avalanche. The transceiver should allow you to localise the victim to within a metre or two, at which point an avalanche probe will be necessary to pinpoint him/her. Transceivers are of little use unless you also have a snow shovel to dig a buried friend out of an avalanche.

A map and compass are also essential items. An altimeter, or a GPS if you are feeling rich and technologically minded, can prove useful, especially in poor visibility.

In terms of clothing it is better to use a multi-layer system so you can adapt your clothing to the conditions. Standard alpine walking/climbing clothing will suffice but with perhaps an extra layer (or two). Even in February it is sometimes possible to be in shorts and t-shirt for the climb but thermals, fleece jackets and a duvet are very welcome as soon as you stop. Two pairs of gloves, a lightweight pair for the climb and standard ski gloves for the descent, make life more comfortable.

Skinning uphill burns calories at an incredible rate so it is important to eat, and even more so to drink regularly. Carry at least 1½ litres of water. Camelback type drinking systems are ideal in spring but the drinking tubes are rather prone to freezing in winter.

For one or two day trips a 35 to 40-litre rucksack is big enough. For longer tours a 45 to 55-litre rucksack is better.

19

MAPS

The sketch maps that I have included in this guide are only designed to give an overall view of the layout of the tours and to help with orientation on the relevant topographical map.

Large-scale maps are essential for ski touring as paths, cairns and even sign-posts are generally covered by the snow. Following other people's tracks is not recommended, unless you are certain that they are going to the same place as you and that the people who made the tracks know what they are doing. In navigational terms, you are on your own!

By far the best and most detailed maps available are the IGN Top 25 series, published by the French national survey at a scale of 1:25,000.

There is also a series of 1:50,000 scale maps, published by Didier Richard. Obviously it is cheaper to buy the larger scale maps and they are ideal for planning, but the extra detail provided by the 1:25,000 maps is invaluable should you get caught in bad weather.

Both map series show a selection of ski tours, some of which are included in this guide. The itineraries marked on the topographical maps are indicative only and the routes that I describe are not always the same as those on the maps.

MOUNTAIN HUTS

This area is very well served by huts. Most of them are run by the French Alpine Club or the Vanoise National

Inside the Refuge du Fond des Fours

Park but there are also a number of private huts.

During the winter months there will only be a small part of each hut open and the warden will not be present. These winter huts usually supply blankets, gas, stoves, pans and eating utensils and have a wood burning fire. The only things that you need to bring are food, matches, candles and a torch, and perhaps a sheet sleeping bag for a bit of extra comfort.

This is the case for all the huts used for the tours in this guide, with the exception of the huts used in the Belledonne. These huts are quite rudimentary; they only supply mattresses and a wood-burning stove for heating. It is necessary to take your own stove, cooking utensils and a sleeping bag.

The toilet facilities tend to be very basic or non-existent in winter. To protect what is a very fragile environment it is a good idea to burn your toilet paper or to take it down with you for disposal.

The unrestricted access to these huts is increasingly being called into question because of the thoughtless minority who abuse the system. It is essential to leave the hut in the state in which you would like to find it and to pay for your night's accommodation. The use of these huts is not free, but rates are very reasonable, usually 10 to 12€ per night. Payment is based on an honesty system; money should be put in the envelopes provided and placed in the letterbox. Without this network of huts, and the facilities they

Skinning back up to the Refuge du Merlet (Alternative Day 4 of the Belledonne tour)

Descent from the Col du Villonet on Day 6 in the Belledonne with
the Puy Gris in the background

provide, ski touring would be much more uncomfortable. Please, do not be among the selfish few who put this service in jeopardy for everyone else.

Many of the huts are guarded during the spring. In these cases there is a warden present and meals are available, either on a half-board or bed-and-breakfast basis. Half board usually costs around 35€, plus drinks. Occasionally, there is no drinking water available. Either you will have to buy bottled water or melt snow. If you only want to pay for your bed (around 10 to 12€) there is usually a small corner where you can cook, often marked *coin hors sac*. When you plan to use a guarded hut you should always book in advance, even if it is only by a few hours. If the hut is full and you have not booked,

you may be turned away. Huts can be booked by phoning the warden. The current phone numbers for the huts used for the tours in this guide are given in Appendix 1. If you book a place in a hut and you cannot get there, please telephone the warden as this will prevent a lot of unnecessary concern about your safety (and possibly avoid food being wasted!).

ACCOMMODATION

As Savoie is a very popular tourist destination there is a wide range of accommodation available. If you want to combine a few days touring with a more traditional resort holiday then it is usually cheapest to go on a package deal booked in the UK.

If you only want to go touring, it is worth staying in the valleys where accommodation is usually cheaper than in the resorts. Another advantage of a valley base is that you can easily change from one area to another for one-day and two-day trips, a real bonus as you will be free to go where the best snow conditions are. This is not such a consideration if you are planning a multi-day trip. In Appendix 2 are listed a few useful publications and the telephone numbers and internet addresses of the main tourist information offices. If you are only planning to spend one or two nights in the valley, the cheapest and often most convenient type of accommodation is in a *gîte d'étape*. These are similar to mountain huts, but are situated beside roads, and are used to dealing with sporty guests.

Outside the French school holidays it is usually possible to find accommodation without booking. During the holidays (all of February and late March to the end of April) booking is essential to avoid disappointment.

BAD WEATHER ALTERNATIVES

If you are unlucky enough to be faced with a period of bad weather making touring impossible and you have had enough of paying 30€ a day to ski in zero visibility in an overcrowded ski-resort, what else is there to do? The answer depends on the time of year.

In the winter months cross-country skiing or snowshoeing can provide entertaining alternatives. There are some excellent cross-country ski areas in Savoie, often amongst the trees and therefore protected from the worst of the weather. Equipment rental and ski passes are much cheaper than for alpine skiing.

Snowshoeing may look like a very pedestrian sport but great fun can be had in forest areas when there is deep snow and the avalanche risk is too high to venture elsewhere. Snowshoes can be rented in most resorts for as little as 8€ a day. Generally there is no point in following sign-posted snowshoeing trails as the snow rapidly gets compacted by the passage of too many people. Get the map out, use a bit of imagination and you will have an excellent day.

In spring it is often possible to go mountain biking or climbing in the valleys in the sunshine when the mountains are buried in cloud. Otherwise, if the weather forecast is abysmal for a few days, remember you are only about a four hour drive from Provence and its much more clement weather.

For more cultural activities, the cities of Grenoble, Annecy, Lyons and Geneva are all within easy reach.

USING THE ROUTE DESCRIPTIONS

The route descriptions give all the information necessary to follow an itinerary, but it must be remembered that the best line to follow will vary depending on the snow conditions.

Below the Col de Morétan into the Pointe de Comberousse in the background (Day 4 of the Belledonne traverse)

Starting and finishing points

The stated heights for these points were taken from the relevant IGN 1:25000 scale maps.

Height gain

The height gain is the difference in height between the starting point and finishing point plus any significant additions due to undulating terrain. The resulting figure has been rounded off to the nearest 10m.

Time

The time required has been calculated on the basis of an average climb rate of 300m per hour, a descent rate of 1000m per hour and a 30-minute break at the summit. Where appropriate, extra time has been allowed for tours that cover long distances or when there is more than one climb. The time required will also depend on snow conditions: it is much quicker to climb and descend in perfect spring snow conditions than in breakable crust!

Orientation

The predominant orientation of the descent(s) is given. This is very important for the timing of your day as

GRADES

EASY
Generally quite gentle slopes but may include very short sections of up to 30°

MODERATE
Longer slopes of up to 30°, possibly including short sections of up to 35°

QUITE DIFFICULT
Slopes of around 35°, possibly including short sections of up to 40°

DIFFICULT
Slopes of around 35 to 40°, possibly including short sections of up to 45°

VERY DIFFICULT
Long slopes of around 40 to 45°

EXTREME
Slopes of above 45°

changes in the qaulity and stability of the snow are related both to the ambient temperature and the warming effect of the sun. Do not hesitate to start early if the descent faces east or south.

The terms right bank and left bank used refer to the true (orographical) right and left banks of rivers and glaciers.

Difficulty

All grading systems are subjective. This is even more so for skiing, as the difficulty of a slope (both for going up and for skiing down) is as much a function of the snow conditions as the gradient. Though it isn't possible to any grading system to take into account snow conditions, the grades here assume these are reasonably good.

The grade descriptions themselves are defined by the gradient of the slope, the length of the steepest sections and the presence of cliffs, or other obstacles, which would make the consequences of a fall more serious. The system adopted, which does not claim any equivalence with any other system used to describe ski tours, uses six grades ranging from easy to extreme (the extreme grade is beyond my own capabilities and thus there are no extreme tours in this guide). Please see the table below for grade descriptions.

The majority of the tours in this book fall into the moderate and quite difficult categories and should be

within the abilities of most competent, experienced ski tourers.

Multi-day tours usually involve slopes with different orientations so you are unlikely to have perfect conditions all the time. It is important to get into the habit of observing the changes in snow conditions during the climb to get a better idea of what is likely to be waiting for you during the descent.

The length of the climb can also contribute to the difficulty of a tour. It is much more difficult to ski well after doing a 1000m climb, especially if you are carrying a heavy rucksack, than when you step off a ski-lift!

N.B. Like all mountain sports, ski touring can be dangerous. Do not over-estimate your abilities; tours should be chosen to suit the weakest member of the party. Embarking on a ski-tour assumes that you have the necessary technical skills to move safely in mountain terrain. If you do not have these skills one of the best ways to learn is to go with a guide.

Side bar text

This give additional information that is not covered by other parts of the description, or to comment on a particular point of interest of the tour.

Itinerary

The itineraries described are not necessarily identical to the ski routes marked on the maps. However, the detailed description of the itinerary and the sketch map are designed to be used in conjunction with the relevant topographical map; the sketch maps give an overview of the tour to help in orientating yourself on the topographical map. Neither the description nor the sketch map can replace the topographical map since snow conditions, changes in the weather, accidents or even fatigue may necessitate major changes to your itinerary.

Alternatives

The Alternatives section, placed at the end of each chapter, suggests a number of ways of making the tour longer or shorter and harder or easier. It also mentions other interesting tours in the same general area.

Other itineraries

This section, identified by the shaded box, locates other itineraries in the same region that may be followed in addition to those described in the tours. Details of the climb, such as the name, the height and the difficulty, are given. Some comments about the nature and features of the climb are also noted.

Skinning up to the Pointe de Combe Bronsin (Day 1) with the Pic du Rognolet and the Grand Pic de la Lauzière in the background

CHAPTER ONE
The Lauzière

INTRODUCTION

The Lauzière is a relatively small massif lying between the entrances to the Tarentaise and Maurienne Valleys, and extending for approximately 35km from Albertville in the north to La Chambre in the south. It is essentially one long line of rocky summits running from north to south, forming the watershed between a series of south-east and north-west facing combes. The highest point of the chain, the Grand Pic de la Lauzière (2829m), is home to the massif's only glacier.

Ease of access, reliable snow conditions throughout the season and the moderate nature of much of the skiing, make the Lauzière one of the most popular ski touring areas in Savoie. Sunny Sundays can see the area invaded by up to 1000 ski tourers and snowshoers. Do not expect to find virgin snow! Fortunately, during the week most of the locals are at work and then it is easier to appreciate the beauty of the mountains and the fantastic skiing that is to be found here.

Tour Profile: Lauzière

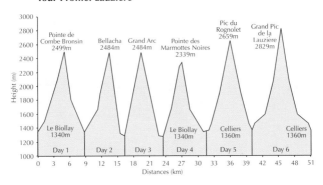

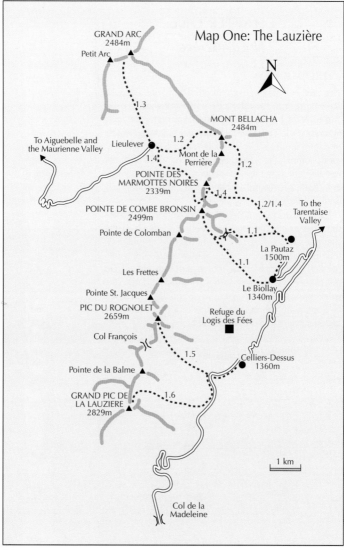

GRAND ARC
2484m
Petit Arc

Map One: The Lauzière

N

1.3

MONT BELLACHA
2484m

To Aiguebelle and
the Maurienne Valley

Lieulever

1.2

1.4

Mont de la
Perrière

1.2

POINTE DES
MARMOTTES NOIRES
2339m

1.4

POINTE DE COMBE BRONSIN
2499m

1.2/1.4

To the
Tarentaise
Valley

Pointe de Colomban

1.1

1.

La Pautaz
1500m

1.1

Les Frettes

Le Biollay
1340m

Pointe St. Jacques

PIC DU ROGNOLET
2659m

Refuge du
Logis des Fées

Col François

1.5

Celliers-Dessus
1360m

Pointe de la Balme

GRAND PIC DE
LA LAUZIERE
2829m

1.6

1 km

Col de la
Madeleine

As the geography of the area does not really lend itself to multi-day tours, I have presented three of the best one-day trips that are to be had. There is also a three-day circuit, which will allow you to combine two great classics with a lesser known tour.

ACCESS

Access is possible both from the Tarentaise Valley, via Le Biollay or Celliers, and from the Maurienne Valley, via Lieulever. All the tours described in this chapter start from the Tarentaise side of the Lauzière. That being said, the direct, and more usual access, for the Grand Arc (Day 3), from the Maurienne Valley to Lieulever, should be used if snow conditions are not stable enough for the traverse of Mont Bellacha.

From Chambéry take either the A43/A430 motorways, or the N90 *route nationale*, to Albertville. From Albertville continue along the N90, towards Moutiers, as far as Feissons-sur-Isère where you pick up the D94 to the Col de la Madeleine. For Le Biollay, turn right just before Villard-Benoit (about 12km from Feissons-sur-Isère). The road is always kept open as far as a hairpin bend just after the village, at 1340m. At the end of March the road is usually opened as far as the hamlet of La Pautaz at 1500m. For Celliers, continue along the D94 as far as Celliers-Dessus at 1360m (21km from Feissons-sur-Isère). By the beginning of May it is usually possible to continue a few kilometres further up the road, thereby gaining another 150m of altitude. By the time the road is open all the way to the Col de la Madeleine it is usually too late for skiing.

Both Le Biollay and Celliers are about an hour's drive from Chambéry.

SNOW CONDITIONS

Good snow conditions can usually be found from the beginning of January to mid-April and sometimes until early May. Because of the relatively low altitude of the area, the snow on south and south-east facing slopes transforms very quickly: spring snow conditions can sometimes be found as early as February.

MAPS

3432 ET Albertville and 3433 ET Saint-Jean-de-Maurienne

RESORT SKIING

The nearest ski resorts are Valmorel (accessible from the Tarentaise Valley) and St.-François-Longchamp (accessible from the Maurienne Valley). The ski areas of these two resorts are linked giving a total of 160km of pistes, most of them green and blue, although there are enough reds and blacks for an interesting day or two. Despite, or perhaps because of, the gentle nature of much of the skiing, these two resorts do not suffer from the 'ski-factory' atmosphere of some of the larger ski areas.

Approaching the summit of the Pointe de Colomban (an alternative route for Day 1). Looking down towards the Combe de Savoie and Chambéry.

Several short ski-tours are accessible from St.-François, some of which use the lifts to reduce the amount of climbing. Among the many possibilities are the Roc Rouge (2375m, moderate), the Col de Sarvatan (2439m, moderate), the Col de la Flachère (2655m, moderate) and the Cheval Noir (2832m, quite difficult). It is very possible to do a short tour in the morning before enjoying a relaxed afternoon on the pistes.

Day 1: The Pointe de Combe Bronsin (2499m)

Starting Point:	Le Biollay (1340m)
Finishing Point:	Le Biollay (1340m)
Height Gain:	1159m
Time:	6 hours
Orientation:	South-east
Difficulty:	Moderate

This is a favourite single-day tour, combining a good circuit with wonderful views and a fabulously sustained but never difficult descent. From the end of March or early April it is possible to drive up to La Pautaz at 1500m, cutting the height gain to 1000m, though you then have to descend by the ascent route.

An early start is essential to ensure good conditions on these very sunny slopes as the Colomban Valley can be quite avalanche-prone after a snowfall. From Le Biollay follow the road to La Pautaz. Turn left and continue towards the south-west, cutting across the hairpins in the forest track, until you come out of the forest. Turn right (west) and follow gentle slopes to the Col du Loup. Descend slightly (this can be a little awkward) then traverse almost due westwards for about 400m before climbing south-east facing slopes to the summit. The summit is the right-hand of the two domes.

The descent follows the sustained south-east facing slopes to the base of the **Colomban Valley**. Stay on the eastern side of the stream to pick up a forest track which is followed back to the parking area.

Day 2: Traverse of Mont Bellacha (2484m): Le Biollay (1340m) to Lieulever (1280m)

Being west facing, there is a good chance of finding powder in winter but it also means that the snow is slower to transform in spring. The climb is about 45 minutes shorter when the road is open as far as La Pautaz.

The only convenient accommodation is at the Relais du Lac Noir, a charming alpine chalet, hidden away at

33

This is a very elegant way to get to the Grand Arc and see a different valley but the descent is steep and extremely sustained; the first 1000m is at an angle of between 30 and 35°. Stable snow conditions are essential.

Starting Point:	Le Biollay (1340m)
Finishing Point:	Lieulever (1280m)
Height Gain:	1140m
Time:	6 hours
Orientation:	West then south-west
Difficulty:	Quite difficult

Starting the climb to Mont Bellacha (Day 2). The pyramid in the background is the Pointe des Marmottes Noires.

the head of a very quiet valley. It is more expensive than a mountain hut (around 55€ for half-board), but still very good value for money. As it only has fourteen beds advance booking is essential.

From **Le Biollay** follow the road to **La Pautaz**. Continue along the road almost horizontally (north-west) to an obvious hairpin bend and a bridge over the river. Leave the road and continue up the base of the valley (north-west) to below the cliffs which bar access to the upper part of the valley. Find a way up to the left of the cliffs; the best line of ascent is very dependent on snow conditions. (The obvious gully just left of the cliffs is a dead-end, closing just before the top). Once above the cliffs, continue due north to the **Col de l'Homme**. From

the col, bear left slightly (north-west) and gain the summit by its south arête.

Descend the north-west arête to a small col at 2350m. The start is very steep and quite exposed. From the col descend sustained slopes due west, towards the Chalet des Rouelles. At the bottom of the valley follow a track to **Lieulever** and the Relais du Lac Noir. Early in the season it is often possible to arrive at the door of the *auberge* on your skis!

Day 3: The Grand Arc (2484m)

Starting Point:	Lieulever (1280m)
Finishing Point:	Lieulever (1280m)
Height Gain:	1200m
Time:	5 hours
Orientation:	South-east
Difficulty:	Moderate

Do not be put off by the intimidating appearance of the south-east face of the Grand Arc when viewed from Mont Bellacha. The slopes are the perfect angle for skiing making this one of Savoie's great ski-touring classics.

From **Lieulever**, follow a track which climbs through the forest past **Les Platières** (1341m). The lower slopes do not hold the snow very long so it is often necessary to carry your skis for this short distance through the forest. Stay on the western side of the stream until you leave the trees. Follow the base of the combe towards the north-west, passing below the **Petit Arc**. At around 2200m, turn towards the north to reach the west arête of the **Grand Arc** not far from the summit.

The usual descent follows the ascent route. However, a more direct, and steeper, line can be taken almost directly from the summit, but take care to avoid the gullies which end in cliffs! Immediately below the cliffs, traverse due east for about 300m then turn right (south-east) to descend below the **Bec d'Aigle**. At an altitude of around 1450m, turn right again (south-west) to rejoin the track which leads back to **Lieulever**.

Day 4: Traverse of the Pointe des Marmottes Noires (2339m): Lieulever (1280m) to Le Biollay (1340m)

Starting Point:	Lieulever (1280m)
Finishing Point:	Le Biollay (1340m)
Height Gain:	1060m
Time:	5 hours
Orientation:	South-east
Difficulty:	Moderate

The Pas de la Mule is not the easiest col to recognise. It is the second depression to the north of the Pointe de Combe Bronsin, just to the left of a quite distinct pyramid (point 2426m). The last thirty metres on both sides of the Pas de la Mule are quite steep and exposed and will often need to be climbed in crampons.

From **Lieulever**, follow the track towards the **Chalet des Rouelles**. The ascent through the forest is a lot easier than it might at first seem, as there is a good track to follow. At the hairpin bend at 1300m, continue south-eastwards for about 150m to pick up the track which leads to the **Chalet de la Perrière** (1680m). Climb almost due east from the Chalet de la Perrière to an altitude of around 1850m. Bear right (south-east) to reach a flat area

Approaching the Pas de la Mule (Day 4)

at 2145m. This is a small lake in summer. The **Pas de la Mule** is due east of this lake. It is best approached via a ramp, which leads in from the south, with the last 30m being done on foot. Traverse the col, descending about 50m on the eastern side, and then head due north to reach the summit of the **Pointe des Marmottes Noires**.

The descent follows south-east facing slopes to 2000m, before joining the ascent route from Day Two. Follow the road back to **Le Biollay**.

Day 5: The Pic du Rognolet (2659m)

Starting Point:	Celliers-Dessus (1360m)
Finishing Point:	Celliers-Dessus (1360m)
Height Gain:	1300m
Time:	6 hours
Orientation:	South then south-east
Difficulty:	Moderate

A justifiably popular tour. However, the final, steep slope below the summit is not usually very easy to ski because of the number of tracks made by people climbing up on foot.

From the car park at the southern end of **Celliers-Dessus**, head due west for a few 100m to join the road. Follow the road to the entrance to the **Ruisseau des Plans Valley** at around 1500m. Follow this valley to about 2300m, and then bear right (north) to reach the final steep slope leading to the summit. Most people leave their skis at a small shoulder about 70m below the summit and do the final section on foot. Descend by the ascent route.

Day 6: The Grand Pic de la Lauziere (2829m)

The easiest route from **Celliers** is to follow the road, as for the Pic du Rognolet, but continue all the way to the entrance to the **Combe de la Valette** (1600m). Follow the left bank of the **Ruisseau de la Valette** to around 2400m, and then bear left (south-west then south) to

You will often find powder in the top section but there is no guarantee that you will have ideal snow conditions for the whole descent. Crampons and an ice axe are essential if you want to reach the summit. The glacier doesn't present any crevasse or serac dangers.

Starting Point:	Celliers-Dessus (1360m)
Finishing Point:	Celliers-Dessus (1360m)
Height Gain:	1470m
Time:	7 hours
Orientation:	North then south-east
Difficulty:	Moderate (except the last 50m which are climbable with crampons and ice-axe: French alpine grade: PD+)

reach the **Glacier des Celliers** at 2500m. The summit can be reached by a short mixed climb but most people are content to reach a highpoint on the arête. Descend by the ascent route.

ALTERNATIVES

DAY 1: The Pointe de Colomban (2455m, moderate), via the Colomban valley, provides a quieter alternative to the Pointe de Combe Bronsin.

DAY 2: If you do not want to traverse Mont Bellacha, the south-east side provides a very pleasant descent, as do the Mont de la Perrière (2436m, moderate) and the Pointe des Marmottes Noires (2339m, moderate).

DAY 3: The Petit Arc (2365m, moderate) is a slightly shorter and easier alternative to the Grand Arc.

DAY 4: The Pas de la Mule is by far the easiest way back to Le Biollay. The other hypothetical routes are either extremely long or extremely steep on one or both sides.

DAY 5: The Portes de Montmélian (2459m, easy), Les Frettes (2527m, easy) and the Pointe Saint Jacques (2531m, quite difficult), to the north of the Pic du Rognolet, are all accessible from the Bridan Valley. The Col François (2495m, easy) provides an alternative to the south.

DAY 6: The Pointe de la Balme (2683m, difficult) to the north of the Aiguille de la Balme, provides an interesting though quite short challenge. Stable snow conditions are essential, as this face can develop some very impressive wind-slabs.

Descent from the Col de Morétan (Day 4)

CHAPTER TWO
The Belledonne

INTRODUCTION

No one who has passed through Chambéry or Grenoble will have failed to notice the Belledonne, a chain of jagged, snowy peaks that runs just east of the valley that connects the two cities. It is one of those areas that few stop to find out about as most drive on to more prestigious destinations. For ski tourers, this is a big mistake. Despite its modest altitude (the highest summit is the Grand Pic de Belledonne at 2978m), the Belledonne has a real high-mountain atmosphere. A week's ski touring amongst these wild and uncompromising peaks can rival the best that many more famous areas have to offer. The lack of easy itineraries and long approaches make this a very committing area for skiing: it is not a place for beginners. Excellent skiers, however, could spend a lifetime in the Belledonne without exhausting all its possibilities.

Apart from the weekends, you are likely to have the mountains to yourself, even during the school holidays when other areas are relatively crowded (this is partly

Tour Profile: Belledonne

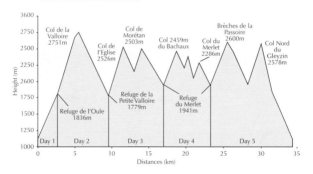

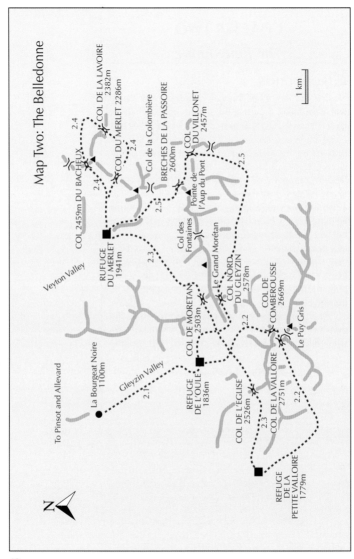

Map Two: The Belledonne

1 km

COL DE LA LAVOIRE 2382m

COL DU MERLET 2286m

2.4

2.4

2.4

Col de la Colombière

BRÈCHES DE LA PASSOIRE 2600m

COL DU VILLONET 2457m

COL 2459m DU BACHEUX

2.4

2.5

Pointe de l'Aup du Pont

2.5

RUFUGE DU MERLET 1941m

Veyton Valley

2.3

Col des Fontaines

Le Grand Morétan

COL DE MORETAN 2503m

COL NORD DU GLEYZIN 2578m

COL DE COMBEROUSSE 2669m

Le Puy Gris

La Bourgeat Noire 1100m

To Pinsot and Allevard

Gleyzin Valley

2.1

REFUGE DE L'OULE 1836m

2.2

COL DE L'ÉGLISE 2526m

2.2

COL DE LA VALLOIRE 2751m

2.3

2.2

REFUGE DE LA PETITE VALLOIRE 1779m

N

42

due to the rudimentary nature of the huts). The huts all have mattresses and a supply of wood for a stove but you need to take a sleeping bag, fire and some cooking utensils with you. Such solitude adds to the wilderness experience but also to the seriousness of ski touring in the area.

The itinerary described here, which should be within the capabilities of most competent skiers, covers the northern part of the Belledonne. This is the wildest and most remote part of the massif but it has the most conveniently located huts. Further south the skiing is just as good but only two of the huts are open in winter and they are better suited to one-day trips than multi-day circuits. The Gleyzin Valley was chosen as the starting point. The road is open all year round and the valley leading up to the Refuge de l'Oule holds the snow longer than some of the other valleys, quite an important consideration given the low starting points. Until at least the beginning of May it is usually possibly to ski down to around 1600m but even with excellent snow conditions it will often be necessary to carry your skis through the forest at the bottom.

Choosing just one tour was not at all easy: there are at least 300 possible ski touring objectives in the Belledonne. Talk to any local ski tourer and they will tell you that there is a life-time of possibilities and that once you have sampled the area's delights you will want to go back time and time again.

ACCESS

Take either the A43/A41 motorways or the N6/N90 *routes nationales* from Chambéry towards Grenoble. Leave the motorway/*route nationale* at Pontcharra and follow signs to Allevard (D925b, turn right onto the D525 at Détrier). Once in Allevard, follow signs to Le Collet d'Allevard, bearing right after about 1½km towards Le Fond de France and Le Pleynet.

Continue along the D525a to Pinsot. Just after the cemetery, a minor road heads off left towards Gleyzin and the hamlet of La Bourgeat Noire.

Driving from Chambéry to the car park takes one hour.

ESCAPE ROUTES

Refuge de la Petite Valloire: descend due west from the hut to the Premier Chalet de la Petite Valloire from where you can pick up the summer path which leads to Le Grand Thiervoz. This takes about 45 minutes.

Refuge du Merlet: the easiest option is to descend westwards, by the Veyton valley, eventually following a track down to the D525a. From the end of March onwards there is likely to be little snow on this track – it is a long walk!

Refuge de l'Oule: again the easiest option is to descend westwards from the hut to reach the Gleyzin valley and the hamlet of La Bourgeat Noire.

Should you have an accident on the eastern side of the chain (eastern side of the Col du Bacheux, Col de la Lavoire, Col du Merlet, Brèches de la Passoire, Col du Villonet, Col Nord du Gleyzin) the easiest way out is to descend to Le Premier Villard or St. Colomban-des-Villards. This is definitely an emergency option as the only easy way to get back to La Bourgeat Noire is by taxi.

Arriving at the Col de Comberousse (Day 2). The col is dominated by the Puy Gris.

SNOW CONDITIONS

Favourable snow conditions can be found from the beginning of January to the end of May, but the best time is March and April. The westerly position of the Belledonne means that it receives more snow than other areas that are more sheltered from Atlantic depressions. The season is thus quite long and it is not unusual for people to be still skiing the north faces in June. Furthermore, despite their low altitude, the steep valley sides deprive the valley floors of sun light until the spring, ensuring many of the valleys hold the snow quite late into the season.

However, the low starting point may make it necessary for you to carry your skis for an hour at the beginning of the tour. At the end of the season, you may have to walk almost all the way to the hut, but the skiing conditions can still be excellent higher up.

The Belledonne is usually one of the first areas to be hit by bad weather and it is not unusual for unstable accumulations of snow to build up. The avalanche risk in this area must not be underestimated.

Crampons can be useful, as even the easiest cols in the area often finish quite steeply, and an ice axe may not be superfluous if the snow is very hard or you are considering some of the steeper variants.

The small glaciers marked on the IGN map are more like *névés* and do not present any crevasse or bergschrund problems.

MAPS

3433OT Allevard

RESORT SKIING

The nearest resort is Le Collet d'Allevard but it is very limited. A better bet is to go to Les Septs Laux. This is a group of three resorts (Le Pleynet, Pipay and Prapoutel) with around 150km of pistes and some excellent off-piste skiing (the north face of the Cime de la Jasse, for example, is magnificent). Les Septs Laux is one of the best value-for-money ski-resorts in the French Alps.

Day 1: La Bourgeat Noire (1100m) to the Refuge de l'Oule (1836m)

This very shaded valley faces north-west and holds the snow amazingly well. It is often possible to ski down to the car park at 1100m when the snowline on the surrounding slopes is at 1500m. Beware of avalanches especially below the Col de Pertuis.

Starting Point:	La Bourgeat Noire (1100m)
Finishing Point:	Refuge de l'Oule (1836m)
Height Gain:	740m
Time:	3 hours
Orientation:	North-west
Difficulty:	Easy

The route is well sign-posted and follows the summer path all the way to the hut. Do not be tempted to continue directly to the hut once above the first rock band at 1600m: access is barred by a very deep and well-hidden gorge. Instead, traverse almost due south to cross the stream (as low as possible as here the snow bridges are most reliable) to reach the hut from the south. The final traverse to the hut is across quite steep slopes. Take extra care if the snow is hard.

Day 2: Traverse of the Col de Comberousse (2669m) and the Col de la Valloire (2751m): The Refuge de l'Oule (1836m) to the Refuge de la Petite Valloire (1779m)

Starting Point:	Refuge de l'Oule (1836m)
Finishing Point:	Refuge de la Petite Valloire (1779m)
Height Gain:	920m
Time:	5 hours
Orientation:	South-west then west then north
Difficulty:	Quite difficult

From the hut there are two possibilities. The most popular option is to climb the steep slopes directly behind the hut to reach a small plateau at around 2100m. This is steep and exposed. However, the second alternative, which involves climbing the west facing slopes across the valley from the hut before traversing south to reach the above-mentioned plateau, is not much easier.

From the plateau, head east-south-east to reach the combe that descends from the Charmet de l'Aiguille. At around 2450m turn right and follow gentler slopes due south to the Col de Comberousse (2669m). Traverse the col and head south-westwards to the Col de la Valloire (2751m). This is the right-hand of two cols, the left-hand one being the Selle du Puy Gris.

Descend the obvious combe, past the Lac Glacé (2449m) and the Lac Noir (2268m), to the Lac Blanc (2124m), and then turn right (north-west) to reach the Premier Chalet de la Grande Valloire (1834m). Traverse northwards across steep slopes (beware of avalanches)

The climb above the hut is not a place to learn how to do kick turns! The ground is steep and there are cliffs below: if the snow is hard, a fall could be very serious. The descent from the Col de la Valloire is magnificent.

Skinning up to the Col de Comberousse with the Pointe de Gleyzin and the Cols de Gleyzin in the background

to the Refuge de la Petite Valloire (1779m). Although generally downhill, this traverse includes two or three short climbs.

Day 3: Traverse of the Col de l'Eglise (2526m) and the Col de Morétan (2503m): The Refuge de la Petite Valloire (1779m) to the Refuge du Merlet (1941m)

Although it is not as difficult as it first looks, the traverse of the Col de l'Eglise is not a pushover. Given hard snow, crampons are likely to be very welcome for the last few metres of the climb. The Col de Morétan further on should not present any real difficulties. This traverse can be divided into two by spending a second night at the Refuge de l'Oule.

Starting Point:	Refuge de la Petite Valloire (1779m)
Finishing Point:	Refuge du Merlet (1941m)
Height Gain:	750m + 350m = 1100m
Time:	6 hours
Orientation:	North-east
Difficulty:	Quite difficult

The Col de l'Eglise, which isn't marked on the 1:25000 map and is well hidden, is found at 2526m on the ridge leading northwards from the Pointes de la Porte de l'Eglise.

From the hut, head due east towards the **Pointes de la Porte de l'Eglise**, turning north-east at around 2350m to climb a narrowing gully which leads to the col at 2526m. (During the first part of the climb the col is hidden by a rocky spur that runs down from the obvious triangular summit to the north of the Pointes de la Porte de l'Église). From the col, descend eastwards then north-eastwards, before contouring round as high as possible (around 2150m) to reach the south-west facing slopes which lead to the **Col de Morétan** (2503m). Put your skins back on your skis and climb to the col. From the col, descend due east then traverse below the **Grand Morétan** to reach sustained north facing slopes to the west of point 2398m. At around 2150m, turn right and

Skinning up to the Col de l'Eglise

make a long descending traverse under the **Crêt du Biais** to the hut. This can almost all be done under gravity if you don't descend too low before starting the traverse.

Day 4: Tour of the Pic Nord du Merlet: The Col 2459m du Bacheux, The Col de la Lavoire (2382m) and the Col du Merlet (2286m)

Starting Point:	Refuge du Merlet (1941m)
Finishing Point:	Refuge du Merlet (1941m)
Height Gain:	520m + 180m + 290m = 990m
Time:	6 hours
Orientation:	East then south then west
Difficulty:	Moderate

This is an elegant way to visit a very inaccessible valley. There are no real difficulties except for the last 50m of ascent to the Col 2459m du Bacheux, which are quite steep.

Skinning up to the Col de Morétan

The Combe du Bacheux has a much wilder atmosphere than its neighbour the Combe du Merlet. The descent from the Col de la Lavoire is superb.

From the hut, head east-north-east to the col (2459m) just north of the **Pic Nord du Merlet**. Descend the eastern side of the col (ensure it is not too late in the day as these slopes see the sun very early in the morning) to the **Lac du Bacheux** at 2200m. Put your skins back on and climb due south to the **Col de la Lavoire** (2382m). From the col, descend sustained slopes southwards into the **Combe du Merlet**. At around 2000m, put your skins on again and climb to the Col du Merlet (2286m). From the col, west facing slopes lead directly back to the hut.

Day 5: Tour of the Grand Morétan: the Brèches de la Passoire (2600m), the Col du Villonet (2457m) and the Col Nord du Gleyzin (2578m)

From the hut, head due south, making a gently rising traverse under the **Crêt du Biais** to reach the **Torrent de la Colombière** (2000m). Cross the stream then head due

The Refuge du Merlet with the Col du Merlet in the background

An early start is essential to have good, safe snow conditions for the descent from the Col du Villonet and the climb to the Col du Gleyzin. This is a long day but well worth the effort. The descent from the Col du Villonet is breath-taking.

Starting Point:	Refuge du Merlet (1941m)
Finishing Point:	La Bourgeat Noire (1100m)
Height Gain:	660m + 610m = 1270m
Time:	7 hours
Orientation:	South-east then south then west
Difficulty:	Moderate

east to pass south of the **Lac de la Colombière** (2197m). Follow steepening slopes due south then east-south-east to reach the **Brèches de la Passoire** (2600m). Descend quite steep south-east facing slopes for about 50m then traverse eastwards to the **Col du Villonet** (2457m). Descend wonderful sustained slopes into **Combe Rousse**, turning right at about 2050m to contour above a line of cliffs. Be careful not to descend too low. Continue by a descending traverse to just below the Rocher Verdane at around 1950m. Put the skins back on your skis and climb east-south-east facing slopes to the **Col Nord du Gleyzin** (2578m). From the col, descend south-west then north-west to the flattish area above the

Below the Grand Morétan, skinning up to the Brèches de la Passoire

Refuge de l'Oule (2100m). Continue north-westwards to descend sustained slopes below the Pic des Grandes Lanches to the **Refuge de l'Oule** (1836m). From the hut retrace your steps from day one, back to La Bourgeat Noire.

ALTERNATIVES

DAY 1: For those with energy to spare it is possible to make a detour on the way up to the hut and ski the enticing couloir which leads to the Col du Pertuis (2365m, difficult). This 600m long slope is at an average of almost 40° and, although not extreme, requires a confident approach.

DAY 2: There are no real alternatives, except for very good skiers who may be tempted by the north-east face of the Pointe de Comberousse (2866m, very difficult, 200m at 40° to 45°).

DAY 3: If you have an extra day to spend in the Refuge de la Petite Valloire it is possible to retrace your steps from Day 2, up to the Lac Blanc, then continue south-east to the Col de l'Arguille (2755m, quite difficult). Another excellent, sustained descent.

DAY 4: The day can be extended by including the north-west face of the Pic Sud du Merlet (2469m, quite difficult).

Instead of returning to the Refuge du Merlet via the Col du Merlet it is possible to go via the Col de la Colombière (2397m, moderate) and descend between the Pic Sud du Merlet and the Crêt du Biais. There is often a small cornice at the top of the eastern side of Col de la Colombière.

Below the Refuge du Merlet, at 'Jerusalem' (Alternative Day 4)

There are many other alternatives possible from the Refuge du Merlet, most of which involve descending northwards into the Veyton valley. The most obvious objectives are: the Grand Charnier, via the Col de la Bourbière, (2561m, quite difficult), the Col du Crozet (2475m, moderate) and the Brèche du Frêne (2700m, quite difficult). The Brèche du Frêne is not marked on the map; it is between the Grand Crozet and the Clocher du Frêne.

A circuit via the Grand Charnier and the Brèche du Frêne, with a night in the Refuge des Férices, would be a great way to continue the tour. The Refuge des Férices is extremely spartan, even by Belledonne standards. There are only six places and there is no wood for the fire, but you are extremely unlikely to find other people there!

DAY 5: The day can be shortened by traversing the Col des Fontaines (2481m). The northern side is very steep (45°) and will almost certainly require crampons and possibly an ice axe. The descent is, however, much more reasonable (moderate).

Skinning up to the Refuge de la Coire (Day 1 of the Beaufortain Tour)

CHAPTER THREE
The Beaufortain

INTRODUCTION

The Beaufortain, an area the French call 'cow-mountains', is perfect ski-touring country. There is something here for everyone, from steep, austere, north-facing gullies to sunny, inviting, south-facing slopes. It is also a fantastically beautiful area with magnificent views of the south face of Mont Blanc to the north and the Vanoise to the south.

The tour that I have chosen covers the central part of the Beaufortain around the Pierra Menta, a spectacular rock spire that has become the symbol for mountain sports in the area. It is a natural focal point for walkers and skiers, and has some excellent rock-climbing.

This five-day tour is ideal for newcomers to ski touring as the days are quite short and the skiing is never very difficult. This allows a relatively leisurely approach to be adopted, but remember it is nearly always better to start too early than too late, both in terms of having good snow for the descent as well as from a safety point of view. The only real difficulty comes from the fact that the huts in

Legend has it that the Pierra Menta was formed when a giant, called Gargantua, kicked a massive lump out of the Aravis Mountains. The resulting hole is the Col des Aravis and the displaced block, the Pierra Menta.

Tour Profile: Beaufortain

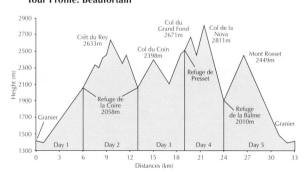

Map Three: Beaufortain

N

Aiguille du
Grand Fond

Pointe de Presset

COL DU GRAND FOND 2671m

3.4

COL DE
LA NOVA
2811m

COL DU BRESSON
2469m

Aiguille
de la
Nova

Peirre Menta

3.3

Roc
de la
Charbonnière

Refuge de la
Balme
2010m

Le Rognais

3.4

Mont Coin

COL DU COIN
2398m

Col de la
Charbonnière

3.5

Pointe de
Plovezan

Refuge de la Coire
2058m

3.3

Pointe de
la Portette

Col du Mont
Rosset

Mont Rosset
2449m

3.2

3.2

3.1

3.5

CRET DU REY
2633m

Col de
Corne Noire
2413m

Pré Pinet

3.2

Pointe de
Combe Bénite

Pont des
Lanches

3.1

Ski-lift car park
1400m

Granier

To Aime

1 km

the Beaufortain are not guarded during the winter so you will have to carry all your food with you: a five-day supply is quite a considerable load! The opposite side of the coin is that, except at weekends, the huts are often empty. Even during the February holidays overcrowding is rarely a problem.

Every year, the area hosts the most prestigious ski-touring race in France; the Pierra Menta-Tivoly. This four day competition is based in Arêches and usually takes place around 10th March. It is an amazing spectacle, attracting several thousand spectators. The feats achieved by the best competitors are very impressive: 10,000m of ascent and descent in a total of around 10 hours. All that being said, if you like peace and quiet while you are in the mountains, it is best to avoid the Beaufortain during this weekend!

ACCESS

From Chambéry, take the A43 and A430 motorways, or the N6 and N90 *routes nationales*, to Albertville. From Albertville, stay on the N90 and follow signs to Moutiers then Aime. Leave the N90 to go through the village of Aime. In the centre of the village, turn left to follow signs to Tessens and Granier (D218). Bear left in the village of Granier to reach a parking area at the foot of the village's ski-lift. From April onwards, it is often possible to continue along the road to the Pont des Lanches. Granier is about 1½ hours from Chambéry.

ESCAPE ROUTES

Refuge de la Coire: descend the valley back to the car park at Granier.

Refuge de Presset/Refuge de la Balme: Descend due south from the Refuge de Presset, turning left (east) at around 2100m to reach the Refuge de la Balme. Continue due east to reach the bottom of the Ormente valley. Follow the valley southwards to reach a good track at Forand. The easiest way to get back to Granier is to follow this track for about 2.5km to where another track, sign-posted to the Refuge de la Coire, branches off to the right. Follow this track, uphill at first, to the Pont des Lanches then to the car park. It is also possible to continue to the cross-country ski centre at Le Pars. This is a very small centre and is generally manned only at weekends. If there is no one there, the nearest civilisation is about 3km down the road at La Bergerie.

SNOW CONDITIONS

The Beaufortain gets more snow than any other area in Savoie and, despite its low altitude, has quite a long ski season. The best conditions for this tour are usually to be found from February to April (or even May in good years). By April, the south-facing slopes at the start and at the end of the tour are likely to be bare so it may be necessary to carry your skis for a short while.

Although this is an easy tour, and often in-condition very early in the season, the avalanche risk should not be underestimated. Several points on the circuit (e.g. Col du Coin, Col de Bresson, Col de la Nova, north side of the Col de Mont Rosset) require stable snow conditions.

MAPS

3532 OT Massif du Beaufortain

RESORT SKIING

The obvious choice for resort skiing is La Plagne. La Plagne has now been linked to Les Arcs, giving a total of over 400km of pistes of all levels.

Day 1: Granier (1410m) to the Refuge de la Coire (2058m)

The climb covers a lot of distance and can seem very long, particularly when carrying a heavy rucksack.

Starting Point:	Granier ski-lift car park (1410m)
Finishing Point:	Refuge de la Coire (2058m)
Height Gain:	650m
Time:	3 hours
Orientation:	South
Difficulty:	Easy

Skinning up to the Refuge de la Coire

Be aware that the steep, sunny slopes below the Pointe de la Portette are prone to avalanche, especially early in the season.

From the north end of the car park, follow the right-hand track (gently downhill at first) to the **Pont des Lanches** (1481m). Cross the bridge and turn left onto another track, which follows the right bank of the stream, to a bridge at 1776m. Cross this bridge and leave the track and cut directly across the hillside, rejoining the track at around 1900m. Follow the track to **Plan Pichu** (1950m), and then bear left (west) to reach the hut.

Day 2: Tour of the Crêt du Rey (2633m)

Starting Point:	Refuge de la Coire (2058m)
Finishing Point:	Refuge de la Coire (2058m)
Height Gain:	280m + 350m + 110 = 740m
Time:	5 hours
Orientation:	All directions
Difficulty:	Moderate

The tour can be lengthened by continuing the descent below the Crêt du Rey towards Véman (1847m) before climbing back to the final col. It is possible to descend the south face directly from the summit of the Crêt du Rey (150m at 40°).

Head due south from the hut, passing the Chalets du Cormet (2090m), to the foot of the north-east ridge of the Crêt du Rey (2332m). (With good snow conditions, this ridge can be climbed on foot directly to the summit, making the tour considerably shorter.) Descend slightly, to the west of the Crête de la Raisse (2414m), towards the Ruisseau de la Pouprezaz (2300m), and then climb up quite steep slopes to the Col de Corne Noire (2413m). From the col, contour round westwards (below the south face of the Crêt du Rey) to reach a sustained south-east facing slope which leads to the summit ridge. The last section along the ridge is usually done on foot. If you don't go to the summit of the Crêt du Rey the circuit is much easier.

From the summit, retrace your steps along the ridge and descend the south-east-facing slope. At around 2400m traverse leftwards to contour round the south ridge. Once around the ridge, keep going westwards to reach the base of a small valley (2350m) that leads to a

Skinning up to the Col de Corne Noire on Day 2 with Mont Coin and the Col du Coin in the background

col just to the east of point 2457m. Traverse this col, from where a final descent of 400m takes you back to the hut.

Day 3: Traverse of the Col du Mont Coin (2398m) and the Col du Bresson (2469m): the Refuge de la Coire (2059m) to the Refuge de Presset (2514m)

The day can be lengthened, and the difficulty increased slightly, by climbing the Mont Coin (2539m, moderate) and descending its north face. Upon reaching the ▶

Starting Point:	Refuge de la Coire (2059m)
Finishing Point:	Refuge de Presset (2514m)
Height Gain:	340m + 370m = 710m
Time:	4 hours
Orientation:	North then east
Difficulty:	Easy

View from the Col du Coin, looking north with Mont Blanc in the background

From the hut, head north-east directly to the **Col du Coin** (2398m). Descend due north, staying to the east of the **Ruisseau du Coin**, to reach the west facing slopes that lead to the **Col du Bresson** at around 2100m. Climb up to the cols (2469m) then turn left to make a slightly ascending traverse to the hut.

◀ Refuge de Presset you will realise it is perhaps one of the most beautifully situated huts in the French Alps.

Day 4: Traverse of the Col du Grand Fond (2671m) and the Col de la Nova (2811m): The Refuge de Presset (2514m) to the Refuge de la Balme (2010m)

Descend slightly from the hut and go around the east side of the lake (2500m). Climb easy slopes, due north, to the **Col du Grand Fond** (2671m). Descend north-eastwards towards two small lakes at around 2430m. The descent follows a shallow combe, just to the west of an obvious cliff (point 2601m). Stay as close to the foot of this cliff as possible if you want to minimise the amount of climbing to the Col

The northern side of the Col du Grand Fond with the Aiguille de la Nova in the background

The views of Mont Blanc and the Aiguille des Glaciers are fabulous. The climb to the Col de la Nova is not as steep as it first looks and the descent on the south side is superb.

Starting Point:	Refuge de Presset (2514m)
Finishing Point:	Refuge de la Balme (2010m)
Height Gain:	170m + 410m + 110m = 690m
Time:	4 hours
Orientation:	North then south
Difficulty:	Moderate

de la Nova. At the end of the cliff (2450m), turn right (east) and traverse towards the foot of the very steep-looking gully that leads to the Col de la Nova. This gully is well protected from the sun but be careful not to start the climb too late in the day. Put the skins back on your skis at around 2400m and climb the gradually steepening gully to the **Col de la Nova** (2811m).

From the col, a magnificent, sustained descent leads to the bottom of the Ormente valley. When the slope eases slightly, at around 1900m, turn right and climb east facing slopes to the **Refuge de la Balme** (2010m).

Day 5: Traverse of the Mont Rosset (2449m): The Refuge de la Balme (2010m) to Granier (1410m)

Starting Point:	Refuge de la Balme (2010m)
Finishing Point:	Granier (1410m)
Height Gain:	440m
Time:	3 hours
Orientation:	South
Difficulty:	Easy

The Mont Rosset is one of the most popular summits in the area as it has a reputation for being very safe, even when the avalanche risk is very high elsewhere. This does not, however, apply to the north side of the Col du Mont Rosset: stable snow conditions are essential here.

From the hut, head south-west for about 300m to reach a north facing combe that leads to the **Col du Mont Rosset** (2332m). From the col it is possible to climb directly eastwards to the summit (2449m); the

slope tends to be very rocky and this sometimes has to be done on foot.

From the summit, descend due south, frequently cutting accross the track leading to the Chalets du Mont Rosset. At **Pré Pinet** (1700m), turn right to follow the track which leads to the **Pont des Lanches** and then to **Granier**.

Below Mont Rosset

ALTERNATIVES

DAY 1: Using the Granier draglift reduces the climb to the hut by about 30 minutes.

DAY 2: The south-west face of the Pointe de Combe Bénite (2575m, moderate). This provides an excellent alternative to the Crêt du Rey.

DAY 3: The day can be made longer, and much harder, by traversing the Roc de la Charbonnière (2738m, difficult) to reach the Ormente valley just above the Refuge de la Balme. Either spend the night here or continue to the Refuge de Presset.

DAY 4: The south-east face of the Pointe de Presset (2858m, quite difficult), which dominates the hut, is not as difficult as it first looks.

DAY 5: The Col de la Charbonnière (2494m, easy) is a slightly longer and more peaceful alternative, although the descent is a little less interesting than that from the Mont Rosset.

A much longer day can be had by descending the Ormente valley to Laval (approx. 1650m), and then skiing the south-west combe of the Pointe de Plovezan (2664m, moderate), before returning to Granier. The descent is superb but stable snow conditions are essential.

A shortened version of the tour (2 days) can be done from the Cormet after the road between Beaufort and Bourg St. Maurice, via the Cormet de Roseland (1967m) is opened in the second week of May. This would make an excellent warm-up trip before doing the Aiguille des Glaciers (see Chapter 12). Day 1: Col de la Nova (2811m, moderate) to the Refuge de la Balme. Day 2: Refuge de la Balme to the Col du Grand Fond (2671m, easy). The tour can also be done in the other direction but the descents are less interesting.

OTHER ITINERARIES

There are many excellent one-day tours around Arêche, making it an ideal resort for combining a few days piste-skiing with a few days touring, but it is not a good base for multi-day tours as there are very few huts. Many of the tours around Arêche are feasible throughout the season from January to April. Especially recommended are: the Legette du Mirantin (2353m, quite difficult), the Roche Plane (2166m, moderate), the Pointe de Riondet (2357m, moderate) and the Grand Mont (2686m, easy).

Skinning up towards the Col des Aiguilles d'Arves (Day 3)

CHAPTER FOUR
Valloire

INTRODUCTION

Valloire has a reputation for being an excellent ski-resort for families; the skiing is varied but not too difficult and the resort has managed to retain a traditional village atmosphere. What is less well known is that the area has some superb ski touring and, thanks to the road up to the Col du Galibier (2642m), a very long season. The Pic des Trois Evêchés (3116m) for example, can provide excellent skiing as late as the middle of June!

Unfortunately, multi-day circuits are difficult due to the absence of huts. Most of the huts marked on the maps are either private and locked (eg. Le Perron d'en Haut) or in ruins (eg. Refuge Carraud, though there are plans to build a new hut here).

The tour that I have chosen is a series of day-trips from the Refuge des Aiguilles d'Arves, the only conveniently situated and usable hut in the area. This tour is of a moderate to quite difficult standard and should be within the capabilities of most competent skiers. In particular, the north faces of the Aiguille d'Argentière

Most of the tours of the area have to be done in one, often quite long, day or require the use of a tent. I have included a few ideas for day and camping-trips in the Alternatives section at the end of the chapter.

Tour Profile: Valloire

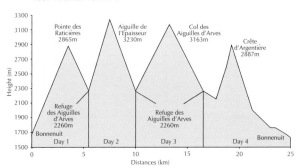

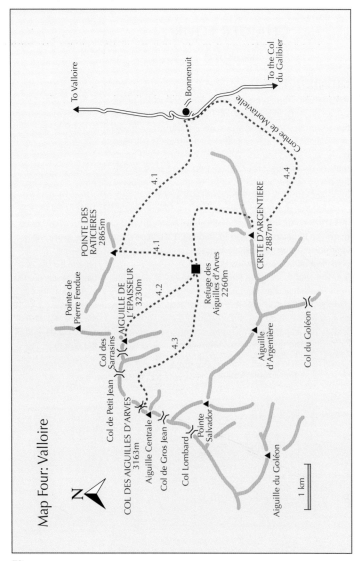

Map Four: Valloire

and the Pointe Salvador boast a number of steep gullies that may be of interest to good skiers.

The Aiguilles d'Arves is one of the most striking and singular mountains in the Alps. The three summit pyramids provide an easily recognisable landmark that can be seen from nearly every mountaintop in Savoie and from as far afield as the Mercantour. The south facing slopes between the Aiguilles d'Arves and the Pointe des Raticières are perfect for skiing: they are very sustained but at an angle that everyone can enjoy. Though the powder doesn't last long on these very sunny slopes, you will often find excellent spring snow. What is more, the Refuge des Aiguilles d'Arves is everything a hut should be: warm, welcoming and not too big. It is also, not surprisingly, extremely popular. At weekends in March and April it is often fully booked a week, or even two, in advance. The best option would seem to be to combine a few days in the hut during the week, when it is usually very quiet, with day-trips or resort skiing at the weekend.

Skinning up to the Pointe 2925m (Alternatives: Valmeinier)

ACCESS

From Chambéry take either the A43 motorway or the N6 *route nationale* towards Modane and Turin. Leave the A43 or N6 at St. Michel de Maurienne and follow signs to Valloire and the Col du Galibier. Go through Valloire and continue to the hamlet of Bonnenuit. From Chambéry to Bonnenuit takes about 1½ hours.

This area is particularly suitable for people who do not have a car as Valloire is well served by public transport. There is a regular train service from Lyons and Chambéry to St. Michel de Maurienne and bus services from St. Michel to Valloire. The local ski-bus goes as far as Les Verneys (approximately 3km from Bonnenuit).

SNOW CONDITIONS

The best snow conditions around the Aiguille d'Arves are usually to be found from February until late April, but conditions can be stable in January. If you are prepared to carry your skis for an hour on the first day, good skiing can usually be had well into May. Both the north-east side of the Crête d'Argentière and the Combe de Mortavieille are notoriously avalanche prone and should be avoided unless the snow-pack is very stable.

MAPS

3435 ET Valloire

RESORT SKIING

The obvious places to go are the linked resorts of Valloire and Valmeinier. Together, these two resorts have a total of 150km of pistes, split reasonably evenly between greens, blues, reds and blacks (although it must be said that the blacks are never particularly steep). There are many excellent one-day tours to be done from both Valloire and Valmeinier, some of which are mentioned at the end of this chapter.

Day 1: Traverse of the Pointe des Raticières (2865m): Bonnenuit (1666m) to the Refuge des Aiguilles d'Arves (2260m)

Starting Point:	Bonnenuit (1666m)
Finishing Point:	Refuge des Aiguilles d'Arves (2260m)
Height Gain:	1200m
Time:	5 hours
Orientation:	South
Difficulty:	Moderate

Ensure you make an early start to have good snow conditions for the descent. During the final part of the climb do not be tempted to traverse under the rock-band just below and east of the summit, even though this looks like a more direct route.

From the car park, cross the river then follow the line of the summer path to the hamlet of **Les Aiguilles** (1845m). This is quite steep but there is generally a good track to follow. At Les Aiguilles, turn right (north-west) to reach **Les Combes** (2245m) then follow the crest of the very blunt ridge (west-north-west) to the summit.

Approaching the summit of the Pointe des Raticières with the Grand Galibier and the Massif des Cerces in the background

Descend the superb sustained slope below the summit to around 2300m, and then contour westwards to cross the **Combe de Puy** and reach the hut.

Note: if you use the ski-bus to get from the centre of Valloire to Les Verneys, you will have to do the climb very quickly to have good, safe conditions for the descent. If you start late, it is always possible avoid the summit by traversing round to the hut at a lower level.

Day 2: The Aiguille de l'Epaisseur (3230m)

The Aiguille de l'Epaisseur is perhaps the epitome of the perfect ski-slope. Almost 1000m at around 30° and so wide that it is almost always possible to find virgin snow.

Starting Point:	Refuge des Aiguilles d'Arves (2260m)
Finishing Point:	Refuge des Aiguilles d'Arves (2260m)
Height Gain:	970m
Time:	4 hours
Orientation:	South-east
Difficulty:	Moderate

Follow the sustained south-east-facing slope behind the hut all the way to the top. Most people ski down the same way they go up. Even on a busy day, it is usually possible to find a peaceful descent route by traversing due east from the summit and descending north-east facing slopes into the Combe du Puy. This can be quite steep, up to 40° or more, depending on the exact line of descent. At the foot of the combe, bear right (south-west) towards the hut.

Day 3: The Col des Aiguilles d'Arves (3163m)

From the hut it is usually easier to descend westwards to

Starting Point:	Refuge des Aiguilles d'Arves (2260m)
Finishing Point:	Refuge des Aiguilles d'Arves (2260m)
Height Gain:	960m + 60m
Time:	4 hours
Orientation:	East and south-east
Difficulty:	Moderate

The skiing is slightly less sustained than for the Aiguille de l'Epaisseur but the surroundings more than make up for that. In fact, very few tours of this degree of difficulty and length can match the Col des Aiguilles d'Arves for scenery and atmosphere. The danger from crevasses on the glacier is negligible.

reach the bottom of the valley at around 2200m, rather than trying to contour round. Follow the Combe des Aiguilles to 2480m then turn right (north) towards the **Col de Petit Jean**. Here there are several possible lines of ascent, the best is the most westerly, just before the steeper slopes and cliffs directly below the col. At around 2850m, turn left (east) and follow a short steeper section to gain the final gentle slopes that lead to the col. Descend by the same route.

View of the summit of the Aiguilles de l'Epaisseur towards Mont Blanc (Day 2)

Day 4: Traverse of the Crête d'Argentière (2887m): The Refuge des Aiguilles d'Arves (2260m) to Bonnenuit (1666m)

Starting Point:	Refuge des Aiguilles d'Arves (2260m)
Finishing Point:	Bonnenuit (1666m)
Height Gain:	890m
Time:	5 hours
Orientation:	South-east
Difficulty:	Quite difficult

The climb to the top of the ridge is steep and very sustained. Later in the season when the south-east facing slopes that lead into the Combe de Mortavieille are bare, a round trip tour, descending by the ascent route, may still be interesting.

From the hut, descend to the **Torrent des Aiguilles**, which is followed down to around 2000m. Make a rising traverse to the south-east to contour round the ridge that runs down from the summit. At around 2150m turn right (south-south-west) and climb very sustained and quite steep slopes to reach the crest of the ridge at around 2600m. Turn right and follow the ridge westwards to a small summit at 2887m.

Descend due south into the **Combe du Claret**, turning east at around 2000m, to reach the bottom of the **Combe de Mortavieille**. Follow the bottom of the valley to cross the river at 1758m. A short climb leads to the road, which you follow back to the car park.

ALTERNATIVES

DAY 1: Climb directly to the hut. It is usually best to follow the line of the summer path to Les Aiguilles, and then continue along the Aiguilles Valley. Following the course of the stream all the way from the bottom can be dangerous either because of avalanches at the beginning of the season or fragile snow bridges at the end.

DAY 2: The Pointe de Pierre Fendu (3037m, moderate) provides a shorter and quieter alternative to the very popular Aiguille de l'Epaisseur.

DAY 3: The Col des Sarrasins (3126m, moderate) and the Col de Petit Jean (3065m, moderate) are both very worthwhile objectives.

DAY 4: The Aiguille d'Argentière (3237m, quite difficult). This is a longer (1450m of ascent) and more difficult, but perhaps even better, tour. From the Crête d'Argentière, descend for 200m into the Combe de Claret. Climb back up to the point 2864m on the Crête Jacques. Traverse horizontally across the Combe de Goléon then follow sustained slopes to the summit, which is gained from the left.

Skinning up to the Pointe 2925m

OTHER ITINERARIES

As mentioned in the introduction, there are several day trips possible from Valloire, Valmeinier or Plan Lachat (below the Col du Galibier). A few examples are given below.

Starting from Valmeinier:

Map:	3535OT Névache, Mont Thabor
Col des Marches:	(2725m, easy)
Point 2925m:	(2925m, moderate). This is the unnamed summit between the Col des Marches and the Pointe de la Sandonnière
Roche Noire:	(3067m, quite difficult). A wonderful summit for skiers as the north-west, west and south-west faces are all skiable

Starting from Valloire:

Grande Chible:	(2932m, quite difficult)
Gros Grenier:	(2911m, quite difficult)

Starting from Plan Lachat:

(follow the Col du Galibier road to 1962m: open at the beginning of May). An excellent few days skiing can be had from a base camp at Les Mottets (2137m):

Maps:	3435 OT Valloire, 3535OT Névache, Mont Thabor
Pointe des Cerces:	(3097m, quite difficult). It is possible to do a circuit, passing by the Refuge des Drayères and the Col des Rochilles.
Grand Galibier:	East face, via the Col Termier (3228m, moderate). The descent via the Glacier de la Clapière is a classic couloir descent (very difficult, 300m at around 45°)
Pic de la Moulinière:	(3073m, quite difficult). A good introduction to skiing couloirs.

CHAPTER FIVE
The Tour of the Mont Thabor

INTRODUCTION

The Massif des Cerces, with Mont Thabor as its centre-piece, is the most difficult area included in this guide to categorise. Apart from the quality of the ski touring, it is an area where superlatives do not really apply. The mountains are neither the highest nor the lowest, the landscape is neither the most rugged nor the gentlest, the weather is neither the best nor the worst… In fact, it is the archetypal transition zone. Lying, as it does, midway between Modane and Briançon, it is geograph-ically part of the Northern Alps, but the influence of the south is already quite strong. The Cerces has a much less austere ambiance than the Vanoise or the Belledonne, for example, but the atmosphere is not quite as Mediterranean as in the Queyras or the Mercantour.

This area is also a political frontier zone, as the number of ruined bunkers and blockhouses around Valfréjus testify. The Vallée Etroite was part of Italy until it was ceded to France at the end of the Second World War. However, the Italian influence remains very strong;

Tour Profile: Mont Thabor

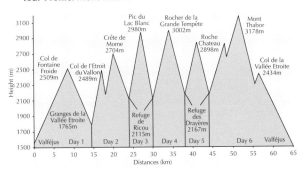

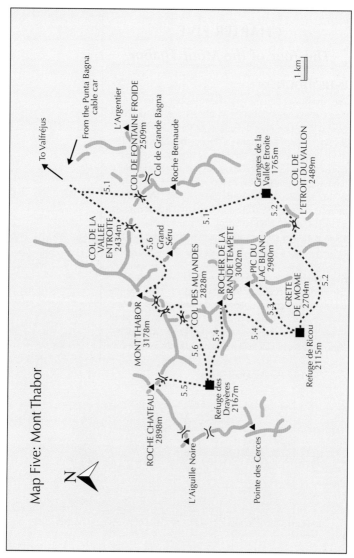

Map Five: Mont Thabor

N

1 km

To Valfréjus

From the Punta Bagna cable car

L'Argentier

COL DE FONTAINE FROIDE 2509m

Col de Grande Bagna

Roche Bernaude

5.1

Granges de la Vallée Etroite 1765m

COL DE L'ETROIT DU VALLON 2489m

5.2

COL DE LA VALLEE ENTROITE 2434m

5.6

Grand Séru

5.1

ROCHER DE LA GRANDE TEMPETE 3002m

PIC DU LAC BLANC 2980m

5.2

COL DES MUANDES 2828m

5.3

CRETE DE MOME 2704m

MONT THABOR 3178m

5.6

5.4

5.4

Refuge de Ricou 2115m

5.5

Refuge des Drayères 2167m

ROCHE CHATEAU 2898m

L'Aiguille Noire

Pointe des Cerces

the two mountain huts in the valley are still run by the Italian Alpine Club and, in winter, the only road access to the valley is via Bardoneccia. The people you meet are as likely to greet you with *buongiorno* as *bonjour*.

The area is perfect for multi-day hut-to-hut tours; there is a good network of huts and many of the summits can be traversed from one valley to the next. The tour that I have chosen includes two quite long days but provides a magnificent circuit. Two of the huts are used for two nights, allowing you to have a more relaxing day before moving onto the next hut. This also means that the tour can easily be shortened if necessary. The huts are very comfortable; two of them even have hot showers. Though this is very nice after a long day's skiing it does detract from the 'away from it all' feeling that is one of the attractions of multi-day ski tours.

ACCESS

From Chambéry, follow the A43 motorway, or the N6 *route nationale*, to Modane. From the centre of Modane follow signs to Valfréjus. Valfréjus is about an hour and fifteen minutes from Chambéry. During the ski season, Valfréjus can be reached using public transport. There is a regular rail service to Modane and buses from Modane to the resort.

ESCAPE ROUTES

There are no very easy or quick escape routes back to Valfréjus from any of the huts. The options described below are the safest means of reaching the valley but they present a bit of a logistical nightmare for getting back to your starting point.

The Refuge de la Vallée Etroite: head south (using a combination of skis, walking and hitch-hiking) to reach Bardonecchia. There is a train service from Bardonecchia to Modane and a bus service (during the ski-season) from Modane to Valfréjus.

The Refuge de Ricou and the Refuge des Drayères: here the situation is even more complicated. The safest route is to head down the Clarée Valley to Nevache.

From Nevache you have to go to Briançon then over the Col de Montgenevre, into Italy, to pick up the train to Modane from either Abbazia or Susa. A more direct route, if circumstances allow, is to traverse the Col de l'Aiguille Noire (north-west of the Refuge des Drayères) and descend the Neuvachette valley to Valloire. There is a regular bus service from Valloire to St. Michel de Maurienne, from where you can get the train to Modane.

SNOW CONDITIONS

Good snow conditions can often be found from February until May although, as usual, the snow-pack is at its most stable in the spring. As the final descent faces north, it is often possible to ski right to the car, even at the beginning of May. This is quite a windy area so wind-crust and wind-slabs are quite common in winter. At the beginning of the season it is not too unusual to find that many slopes have been stripped bare by the wind: January is generally not a good time for touring in this area.

MAPS

3535 OT Névache/Mont Thabor

RESORT SKIING

The obvious choice for resort skiing is Valfréjus. There are 52km of pistes catering for all levels. The Argentier (3046m, moderate) provides a good short tour that is accessible from the lifts.

The resort of La Norma, which is a few kilometres further east, has 65km of pistes. A classic ski tour from La Norma is the Belle Plinier (3086m, quite difficult), which offers 1000m of sustained but not too difficult skiing.

Both these resorts face north and often have good powder snow.

Day 1: Traverse of the Col de Fontaine Froide (2509m): Valfrejus (1548m) to Les Granges de la Vallée Etroite (1780m)

Starting Point:	Valfréjus (1548m)/Fontaine Froide (2050m)
Finishing point:	Les Granges de la Vallée Etroite (1780m): Refuge I Tre Alpini or Refuge I Re Magi
Height Gain:	460m (from Fontaine Froide)
Time:	3 hours (from Fontaine Froide)
Orientation:	South
Difficulty:	Easy

Take the **Punta Bagna cable car** and descend a red piste to the **Pas du Roc**. From here, a blue piste leads towards **Le Jeu** (2160m). Continue along this piste until you reach a right-hand hairpin bend, about 600m after Le Jeu (2060m). Leave the piste and head almost due north,

During the ski season, (up until the middle of April) the road is closed at Valfréjus making the climb to Fontaine Froide extremely long. The route follows a narrow green ski-run for almost 5km. However, for approximately 10€, you can buy a *randonneur* ski-pass, which allows you to take the Punta Bagna gondola and descend to Fontaine Froide, via the Pas du Roc.

Below the Col de Fontaine Froide

At the end of the season, it is often possible to drive much further up the road from Vlafréjus towards Le Lavoir.

along a shallow combe, to reach the **Col de Fontaine Froide** (2509m).

From the col descend south-west to the **Grosse Somme** (2326m) then due south, to the **Plaine de Tavernette** (2196m). Cross over to the western side of the **Vallon de Tavernette** and continue due south towards the **Pont de la Fonderie** (1910m). Where the slope steepens, at around 2150m, the descent is made more complicated by a line of small cliffs. The easiest way through them is to the west. From the Pont de la Fonderie, a good track leads to the **Granges de la Vallée Etroite** (1708m).

Day 2: Traverse of the Col de l'Etroit du Vallon (2489m) and the Crête de Mome (2704m): The Granges de la Vallée Etroite (1780m) to the Refuge de Ricou (2115m)

The first descent, from the Col de l'Etroit du Vallon, is quite steep and exposed. In spring this will have to be done early in the day, while the snow is hard, in order to have reasonable conditions for the climb to the Crête de Mome. The Refuge de Ricou is very small so advance booking is essential.

Starting Point:	The Granges de la Vallée Etroite (1780m)
Finishing Point:	Refuge de Ricou (2115m)
Height Gain:	710m + 550m = 1260m
Time:	7 hours
Orientation:	South-west then north-west
Difficulty:	Quite difficult

From the hut, follow the path that zigzags through the trees on the right bank of the **Combe de la Miglia**. Continue along this path to the **Col des Thures** (2194m). From the col, follow the right bank of the Riou de Thures up to a large flat area at around 2280m. Continue due west to go around the north side of **Point 2461m**. From here, easy slopes lead to the **Col de l'Etroit du Vallon** (2489m). At the col, remove your skins and descend, at first hard left (south-west), to avoid some very steep

Refuge de Ricou

ravines, then west, to reach the **Chalets du Vallon** (2174m). The first part of this descent is quite exposed – be careful!

Put your skins back on and climb due west, steeply at first, to reach the **Lac Noir** (2391m). Pass a rock band on the right (north) then head south past a small lake at 2501m. With good snow conditions, it is possible to climb directly to this small lake. After the lake, follow a small valley, first due west and then north-north-east, to reach a col at 2704m.

Descend towards the west-south-west for 500m until you reach the **Chemin de Rond** (2250m). The easiest way to reach the hut is to follow this track, for about 1½km, to just before the Ruisseau du Lac Laramon and then descend west-facing slopes to the hut.

Day 3: The Pic du Lac Blanc (2980m)

From the hut, head due north to reach the **Ruisseau de la Recare** at around 2300m. Follow the valley past two small lakes to a third at 2725m. From here steeper slopes lead directly to the summit. A slightly easier, but longer,

A more relaxing day which can be shortened even further by stopping at the Crête des Gardioles (2935m) or the Col du Grand Cros (2848m). The views of the Massif des Ecrins are stunning.

Starting Point:	Refuge de Ricou (2115m)
Finishing Point:	Refuge de Ricou (2115m)
Height Gain:	865m
Time:	4 hours
Orientation:	South then south-west
Difficulty:	Moderate

way of reaching the summit is to continue to the **Crête des Gardioles** (2935m) then follow the south arête of the **Pic du Lac Blanc** to the summit. Descend by the same route.

Day 4: Traverse of the Rocher de la Grande Tempête (3002m): The Refuge de Ricou (2115m) to the Refuge des Drayères (2167m)

There are a number of wide gullies, which lead from the Lac de la Cula to the Crête des Muandes, none of which present any real difficulties. The climb can be made by any one of these gullies.

Starting Point:	Refuge de Ricou (2115m)
Finishing Point:	Refuge des Drayères (2167m)
Height Gain:	887m
Time:	5 hours
Orientation:	West
Difficulty:	Moderate

From the hut, head due north for about 1½km to go round the **Crête de la Cula** at around 2350m. Turn right (north-east) and continue to the **Lac de la Cula** (2450m). Turn left (north) and follow a wide gully to the **Crête des Muandes** and an obvious small col at 2860m. From here there are two possibilities: either follow the ridge directly to the summit, or descend the north side of the col for about 50m and gain the summit from the north-west. The last 100m may have to be done on foot, depending on snow conditions.

Skinning up the Clarée Valley towards the Refuge des Drayères
with the Pointe des Cerces in the background

Descend west-facing slopes to the **Lac Rond** (2446m). Continue due west to reach the **Ravin des Muandes** at around 2300m. Cross the stream and follow the right bank to the hut.

Day 5: The Roche Château (2898m)

This a relatively short day, on an almost perfect slope; it's a shame it isn't longer. However, it allows your legs to recover a little before attacking the Mont Thabor.

Starting Point:	Refuge des Drayères (2167m)
Finishing Point:	Refuge des Drayères (2167m)
Height Gain:	730m
Time:	3½hrs
Orientation:	South
Difficulty:	Moderate

From the hut, head north-east to reach the **Vallon de Lau**. At around 2650m, bear right to reach the **Col de la Madeleine** (2841m). Follow the ridge north-westwards to the top. Descend by the same route.

Day 6: Traverse of the Mont Thabor (3178m): The Refuge des Drayères (2167m) to Valfréjus (1548m)

This is a very long day so, bearing in mind the orientation of the first part of the descent, an early start is essential. The climb to the summit takes most parties at least 4 to 4½hrs.

Starting Point:	Refuge des Drayères (2167m)
Finishing Point:	Valfréjus (1548m)
Height Gain:	660m + 580m + 30m = 1270m
Time:	8 hours
Orientation:	South-east then north
Difficulty:	Moderate

From the hut, follow the **Torrent de Brune** then the **Ravin des Muandes** to the **Lac des Muandes** (2580m). Turn left (north) then, at around 2650m, bear right to reach the

Col des Muandes (2828m). From the col, descend due east to gain the base of the combe (2650m). Put your skins back on and climb northwards to reach the **Col de Valmeinier** (2850m). (It is possible to contour round to the Col de Valmeinier, passing under the Roche du Chardonnet, but this not to be recommended unless the snow is very stable.) From the Col de Valmeinier, traverse north-westwards to reach the **Col de la Chapelle** (2943m). Continue towards the north-west, to go around the south arête of the **Mont Thabor**, and then, at around 3050m, turn left (north) to reach the summit.

From the summit, descend due south to around 2800m, and then bear left to reach the **Col des Méandes** (2727m). The col is actually much closer to the foot of the **Grand Séru** than would appear from the map. Do not try to go left too soon, the Col des Méandes is the only passage through the cliffs. Follow a shallow depression under the north face of the Grand Séru, to an altitude of around 2550m, then head north to reach the **Lac du Peyron** (2440m). There are some quite large cairns, which should be visible unless there is an exceptional amount of snow. From the lake, contour round to the north, losing as little height as possible, to reach the bottom of the valley that leads to the **Col de la Vallée Etroite** (2434m), at around 2400m. Put your skins back on for the short climb to the col. From the col descend north-eastwards to reach **La Losa** (2099m), **Le Lavoir** (1923m) and then **Valfréjus** (1548m). Do not be tempted to descend into the bottom of the valley, as the valley sides are often very steep and impassable.

ALTERNATIVES

DAY 1: The day can be lengthened by taking in the Col de Grand Bagna (2990m, quite difficult), the obvious north-west facing slope on your left just before arriving at the Col de Fontaine Froide. Stable snow conditions are essential for this tour. The best way to do this col would be to add an extra day to the tour and spend a night at the Refuge du Thabor. From the hut, descend to the Col de la Vallée Etroite. Descend the south side of the col, heading east-south-east towards the Cime de la Planette. From around 2350m, climb back up to the Col de Fontaine Froide and then to the Col de la Grand Bagna. This could be done either at the beginning or the end of the tour.

DAY 2: The hut can be reached, more directly, via the Pic du Lac Blanc (2980m, moderate), allowing the tour to be shortened by a day. The route passes by the Maison des Chamois (north-west of the hut), goes around the Pointe de l'Enfourant and over the Col du Vallon. After a short descent (no need to remove your skins) traverse across the Lac Blanc and climb a short ridge to reach the Crête des Gardioles then head north-west to the summit. This is still quite a long day as the climb takes around 4hrs.

DAY 3: There are no real alternatives.

DAY 4: If snow conditions on south faces are better than on north faces, it is possible to descend back to the Lac de la Cula and then head west-south-west to reach the Refuge de Laval. It takes about an hour to skin up to the Drayères hut from here.

DAY 5: The Pointe des Cerces (3097m, difficult) via the Ruisseau des Sagnes Froides and the Lac Sorcier. This is a magnificent ski tour but much more difficult than the other tours described above.

DAY 6: A slightly longer day, but with a more interesting descent at the end, can be had by traversing the Passage Ste. Marguerite (2586m) instead of the Col de la Vallée Etroite. From La Baume (2416m) head due north, to the east of Chateau Léger, to reach a small col. Descend past the Refuge du Thabor and follow the left bank of the river to La Losa.

The shortest way back to Valfréjus (although it isn't much shorter!) involves traversing the Col des Muandes, descending south-eastwards to the Pont de la Fonderie, in the Vallée Etroite, and then climbing up to the Col de la Vallée Etroite. This route involves about 1100m of climbing.

CHAPTER SIX
The North Vanoise

INTRODUCTION

The Vanoise, home to the Grande Casse, the highest summit in Savoie, became France's first national park when it was set-up in 1963. The park, which covers almost 530 sq km, has an international reputation for its beautiful scenery and wildlife, for good walking in summer and for ski touring in winter. The Vanoise is far too big to be explored in a single ski tour, so for the purposes of this guide, it has been divided into three sections: the Champagny Valley, which lies to the north of the Grande Casse, the Vanoise Glaciers (Chapter 7), which lie to the south, and the area around Val d'Isère (Chapter 8), which lies to the east. The two highest summits, the Grande Casse and Mont Pourri, are described as ski mountaineering routes in Chapter 12.

Below the Dôme des Pichères (Day 2) with the Roche Noire, the Aiguille de la Grande Glière and the Col du Tougne in the background

Tour Profile: North Vanoise

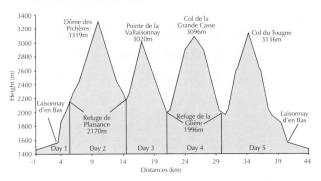

This chapter covers the Champagny Valley, one of the most beautiful valleys in the French Alps. The southern side of the valley is composed of a line of forbidding rocky summits and tormented glaciers that, at first sight, would seem to be more the domain of the mountaineer than the skier. Fortunately, there are one or two chinks in the armour that allow the competent skier to penetrate this magical world (namely, the Col de la Grande Casse and the Col du Tougne). The atmosphere of the more open northern side of the valley is much less austere. These gentler slopes, home to large herds of chamois and ibex, encourage a more relaxed approach to skiing. It is difficult to resist the temptation to linger at the summit, while waiting for the best moment to descend, and enjoy the sunshine and breathtaking views.

The tour that I have chosen, is of a moderate standard and would provide an ideal introduction to high-mountain ski touring. It uses two huts, neither of which is guarded during the ski-touring season. The Refuge de Plaisance is easily accessible from La Plagne and therefore often quite popular. It can be a little cramped when it is busy, so it is not a bad idea to arrive early to be sure of finding a place to sleep. The Refuge de la Glière is almost the perfect mountain hut. It is

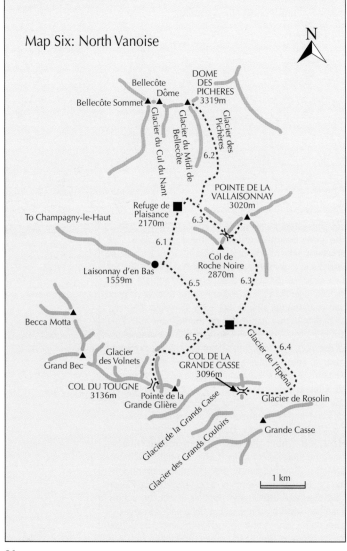

Map Six: North Vanoise

N

Bellecôte
Dôme
DOME
DES
PICHERES
3319m

Bellecôte Sommet

Glacier du Cul du Nant

Glacier du Midi de Bellecôte

Glacier des Pichères

6.2

POINTE DE LA
VALLAISONNAY
3020m

Refuge de
Plaisance
2170m

To Champagny-le-Haut

6.3

6.1

Col de
Roche Noire
2870m

6.3

Laisonnay d'en Bas
1559m

6.5

Becca Motta

6.5

Glacier de l'Epéna

6.4

Grand Bec

Glacier
des Volnets

COL DE LA
GRANDE CASSE
3096m

COL DU TOUGNE
3136m

Pointe de la
Grande Glière

Glacier de Rosolin

Glacier de la Grands Casse

Grande Casse

Glacier des Grands Couloirs

1 km

*The Col de la
Grande Casse
(Day 4)*

small, well equipped without being luxurious and
wonderfully situated at the foot of the Aiguille de
l'Epéna. It is also much quieter than the Plaisance hut.

Although never technically difficult, the tour reflects
the contrasting ambience of the two sides of the valley:
the open slopes of the Dôme des Pichères are the
antithesis of the narrow defile that is the Col de la
Grande Casse. It can be done in either direction but,
assuming that the avalanche risk for the climb to the
Refuge de Plaisance is not too high, the most logical
direction is to go to Plaisance then Glières, thus leaving
the most spectacular tours to the end.

ACCESS

From Chambéry, follow the A43 and A430 motorways
or the N6 and N90 *routes nationales* to Albertville, and
continue along the N90 to Moutiers. In Moutiers, take
the D915 to Bozel, and then turn left onto the D91 to
Champagny-en-Vanoise. From Champagny-en-Vanoise
the road continues to Champagny-le-Haut. In winter you
can drive as far as Le Bois; in spring the road continues
to Le Laisonnay d'en-Bas.

SNOW CONDITIONS

Good snow conditions can be found from January until June. However the avalanche risk during the winter months should never be underestimated. The snow on the sunny slopes of the Dôme des Pichères and the Pointe de Vallaisonnay transforms quite quickly in the sun whereas the Col de la Grande Casse is nearly always in shadow so powder (or wind crust!) lasts a lot longer.

MAPS

Three 1:25,000 scale maps are needed for this area.

    3532 ET Les Arcs – La Plagne
    3534 OT Les Trois Vallées
    3633 ET Tignes, Val d'Isère

RESORT SKIING

The resort of Champagny-en-Vanoise forms part of the La Plagne/Les Arcs ski-area.

For those looking for a smaller, quieter resort, Pralognan-la-Vanoise (about 10km from Champagny-en-Vanoise) has 32km of pistes. Champagny-le-Haut has some very good cross-country skiing. During the ski season, there is a regular shuttle bus service between Champagny-en-Vanoise and Champagny-le-Haut.

Day 1: Le Bois (1470m) to the Refuge de Plaisance (2170m)

Starting Point:	Champagny-le-Haut/Le Bois (1470m)
Finishing Point:	Refuge de Plaisance (2170m)
Height Gain:	700m
Time:	3 hours
Orientation:	South
Difficulty:	Easy

The west facing slopes of the Couloirs du Mollard are extremely avalanche prone, especially early in the spring and thus the climb to the hut should be done early in the morning.

Follow the road from **Le Bois** (1470m) to **Le Laisonnay d'en Bas** (1559m). This is a groomed cross-country ski

98

trail. It is debatable whether this section is easier with skins on your skis or without. Turn left and follow the left bank of the obvious gorge of the **Ruisseau du Py**, quite steeply at first, to the hut.

From April onwards, it is possible to drive to Le Laisonnay d'en Bas and it is also usually necessary to carry your skis up to around 1900m.

Avalanches sometimes have a beneficial effect, as they transport snow into the bottom of the valley thus maintaining a reasonable snow cover quite late into the season.

Day 2: The Dôme des Pichères (3319m)

Starting Point:	Refuge de Plaisance 2170m
Finishing Point:	Refuge de Plaisance 2170m
HHeight Gain:	1149m
Time:	5 hours
Orientation:	South
Difficulty:	Moderate

From the hut head south-east for a short distance to go around a line of small cliffs at 2300m. After passing the

Skinning up to the Dôme des Pichères with the Grande Casse in the background

The views of the Mont Pourri and the Grande Casse are superb. The descent is never difficult but always interesting.

cliffs turn northwards to reach **Le Plan Séry** at around 2458m. Bear right (north-east) to climb the **Grand Tuf du Plan Séry**, reaching a small lake at 2784m. From the lake, head due north to reach the **Glacier des Pichères** at about 3000m. Continue due north to around 3200m, and then turn left to reach the summit from the south-east. Descend by the same route.

Day 3: Traverse of the Pointe de la Vallaisonnay (3020m): The Refuge de Plaisance (2170m) to the Refuge de la Glière (1996m)

This day offers a very direct and quick ascent. Again the views, especially of the Grande Casse, are superb. On top of this modest summit you really feel that you are in the middle of things.

Starting Point:	Refuge de Plaisance (2170m)
Finishing Point:	Refuge de la Glière (1996m)
Height Gain:	850m
Time:	4 hours
Orientation:	South
Difficulty:	Moderate

Retrace your steps from Day 2 to go round the first line of cliffs. At around 2300m, head south-east to reach the **Col de Roche Noire** (2870m). From the col, follow the south-west ridge to the summit of the **Pointe de Vallaisonnay**. The last 50m below the summit are usually too rocky to be skied.

From the summit, go back to the **Col de Roche Noire**, and then head almost due south to reach a track at around 2300m. Follow the line of this track, south-west, to reach a cross at 2235m. The hut is due south of this cross. This is very undulating terrain and the hut is quite well hidden so choosing the best line of descent is not easy. The summit of the Aiguille de l'Epéna is a good point to aim towards.

Day 4: The Col de la Grande Casse (3096m)

Starting Point:	Refuge de la Glière (1996m)
Finishing Point:	Refuge de la Glière (1996m)
Height Gain:	1100m
Time:	6 hours
Orientation:	East then north then west
Difficulty:	Moderate

This is perhaps the most grandiose easy ski tour in the region. During the ascent you will find it very hard to believe that there could be an easy passage between the imposing rock walls of the Aiguille de l'Epena and the Grand Casse.

From the hut, climb due east to reach the **Lac de la Glière** (2040m). Cross the lake and turn right (north) to follow first a slight combe and then its left ridge to reach the **Glacier de Rosolin** at around 2700m. Keep heading due north to just below the very impressive north face of the Grande Casse. At around 2900m, turn right (east) and traverse above the seracs to reach the col. Descend by the ascent route.

Skinning up to the Col de la Grande Casse with the Roche Noire and the Pointe de Vallaisonnay in the background

Day 5: The Col du Tougne (3136m): The Refuge de la Glière (1996m) to Le Bois (1470m)

Starting Point:	Refuge de la Glière (1996m)
Finishing Point:	Champagny-le-Haut/Le Bois (1470m)
Height Gain:	1220m
Time:	6 hours
Orientation:	North then north-west
Difficulty:	Moderate

This route is the easiest way to the ridge that runs from the Grand Bec to the Aiguille de l'Epéna. From the hut, the ascent appears a little complicated and even delicate in places but it is not nearly as bad as it looks.

From the hut, descend due west (along the line of the track if this is visible) to cross the stream (bridge at 1920m). Continue along the track (west-south-west) to reach an altitude of around 2100m. Turn left (south) and climb towards the **Pointe de la Grande Glière**. At 2600m, bear right (west) to make a rising traverse across sustained slopes, which lead to the **Glacier de la Roche du Tougne** (2700m). Follow the glacier (due north), making a slight detour to the right at around 2800m to avoid some crevasses. When you reach the point 3136m, where three arêtes come together, you will see this has a much better view than the col itself.

Descend by the ascent route back to the bridge. At the bridge, turn left (west) and follow the valley floor to **Le Grand Chalet** (1890m), where you pick up an obvious track that leads back to **Le Laissonay d'en Bas** and **Le Bois**.

ALTERNATIVES

DAY 1: The Refuge de Plaisance can be reached from the ski-lifts at La Plagne. Obviously, this option poses the problem of getting back to La Plagne at the end of the tour. The easiest solution is to start from Champagny-en-Vanoise, but you need to take several lifts to end up at the top of the Col draglift. It is a good idea to be on the first lift in the morning as the final descent faces due south.

DAY2: Though the Dôme de Bellecôte (3389m, quite difficult) and the Sommet de Bellecôte (3417m, difficult) tend to be more crowded than the Dôme des Pichères (becuase of their easy access from La Plagne), they provide excellent descents.

DAY 3: The Roche Noire (2931m, moderate) is 90m lower than the Pointe de Vallaisonnay. It has the added advantage that you can ski directly from the summit, but the view is not quite as spectacular.

DAY4: The Dôme de Pramecou (3081m, quite difficult) is more difficult but less spectacular than the Col de la Grande Casse.

DAY5: There are no good alternatives.

OTHER ITINERARIES

The Grand Bec (3398m, quite difficult) and the Becca Motta (3045m, moderate), via the Refuge du Plan des Gouilles. The Grand Bec is a classic (and very popular) spring season tour. The Becca Motta is much less frequented and can be in condition quite early in the season.

Skinning up to the Col d'Aussois (Day 4) with the Pointe de l'Echelle in the background

CHAPTER SEVEN
The Glaciers de la Vanoise

INTRODUCTION

Without a shadow of a doubt, the Vanoise Glaciers are the jewel in the crown of the Vanoise area. Stretching from the Grande Casse in the north to the Dent Parrachée in the south, the glaciers form the centrepiece of the Vanoise National Park and have therefore been protected from the encroachments of neighbouring ski-resorts. The area has long been known as the central part of a set of three French ski-touring areas that includes the Mont Blanc massif to the north and the Ecrins massif to the south.

The glaciers form a high plateau, from which rise a number of *dômes*, culminating in the Dôme de l'Arpont at 3599m. The glaciers are surrounded by steep, rocky summits, such as the Dent Parrachée and the Pointe de l'Echelle, which provide a spectacular contrast to the wide-open spaces of the plateau. Floating through this breathtaking scenery on a cloud of perfect powder is an unforgettable experience.

Tour Profile: Glaciers de la Vanoise

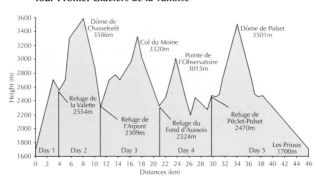

105

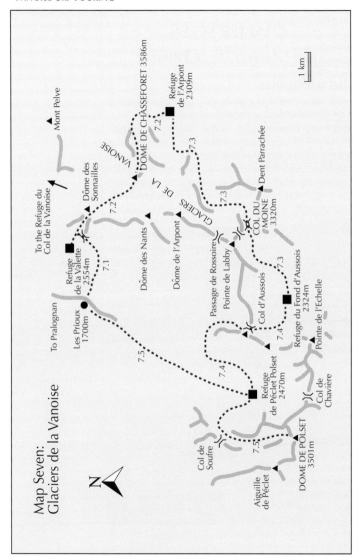

Map Seven:
Glaciers de la Vanoise

N

1 km

Mont Pelve

DÔME DE CHASSEFORET 3586m

Refuge de l'Arpont 2309m

7.2

7.3

To the Refuge du Col de la Vanoise

Dôme des Sonnailles

VANOISE

7.2

Dent Parrachée

GLACIERS DE LA

7.3

Dôme des Nants

Dôme de l'Arpont

COL DU MOINE 3320m

Refuge de la Valette 2554m

7.1

Passage de Rossoire

Pointe de Labby

Col d'Aussois

7.3

To Pralognan

Les Prioux 1700m

7.5

Refuge du Fond d'Aussois 2324m

7.4

Pointe de l'Echelle

Refuge de Péclet Polset 2470m

7.4

Col de Chavière

7.5

Col de Soufre

7.5

DÔME DE POLSET 3501m

Aiguille de Péclet

There are several ways to get onto the plateau, although not all of them are easy. The most popular round-trip tour is the Dôme de Chassefôret from the Refuge du Col de la Vanoise as, though long, it is easy and presents very few problems in terms of crevasses and seracs. In the spring, and even in winter if the conditions are reasonable, the Refuge du Col de la Vanoise is often packed with skiers. However, if you have the time and the right weather conditions, the best way to appreciate the Vanoise Glaciers is through doing a multi-day circuit. This enables you to sample the delights of the different combes, valleys and summits that make up this magnificent area. The circuit described is the easiest five-day circuit in the area though some of the climbs are quite long. Most of the time you will be on a glacier, so as well as being a competent skier it is essential to have the skills required to move safely over glaciated terrain.

The tour uses four huts: Valette, Arpont, Fond d'Aussois and Péclet–Polset. The first three of these huts are never guarded during the ski season, so you will have to take all your own food. Furthermore, the Fond d'Aussois hut has almost no cooking pots so bring some along. The dormitory in this hut is under the dining room: there is a trap door in the corner, to the left of the main door! The Péclet–Polset hut is guarded during March and April.

ACCESS

From Chambéry follow the A43 and A430 motorways or the N6 and N90 *routes nationales* to Albertville, and then continue along the N90 to Moutiers. In Moutiers take the D915 to Bozel then Pralognan-la-Vanoise. If the road is open (usually from mid-April onwards), continue through Pralognan to the car park at Les Prioux. From Chambéry to Les Prioux takes about 1½hrs. If the road is closed, the best way to start the tour is via the Refuge du Col de la Vanoise (see the Alternatives section at the end of the chapter).

ESCAPE ROUTES

Refuge de la Valette: descend back to Les Prioux.

Refuge de l'Arpont: The quickest way is to descend south-south-east to the Chapelle St. Laurent then Le Mont. Turn left (east) to follow the track down to Le Chatelard and the road that leads to Termignon.

Refuge du Fond d'Aussois: head south-east, along the flat valley floor, to the Plan d'Amont reservoir. Follow the west bank to the dam where you pick up the road to Aussois.

Refuge Péclet-Polset: descend back to Les Prioux via the Doron de Chavière Valley.

The escape routes from the Arpont and Fond d'Aussois huts are for real emergencies only. Getting back to your start point, from either Termignon or Aussois, would be a logistical nightmare: taxi or bus to Modane, train to Albertville and then to Moutiers and taxi or bus to Pralognan. Even if you are lucky with connections, the journey would probably take at least 6hrs!

SNOW CONDITIONS

Good snow conditions can be found from March until the end of May. During the winter months the snow, especially on the steeper slopes, can be very unstable and the snow bridges over crevasses may be very fragile. In spring, the lower slopes are often bare but it is still possible to have excellent snow conditions higher up.

MAPS

3534 OT Les Trois Vallées

RESORT SKIING

Pralognan-la-Vanoise has 32km of pistes encompassing all levels of difficulty. The Three Valleys resorts of Courchevel and Meribel are easily accessible from Bozel and Brides-les-Bains.

Day 1: Les Prioux (1700m) to the Refuge de la Valette (2554m) via the Col des Thurges (2679m)

Starting Point:	Les Prioux (1700m)
Finishing Point:	Refuge de la Valette (2554m)
Height Gain:	1000m
Time:	4 hours
Orientation:	West
Difficulty:	Easy

A footpath leaves the road to the hamlet of **Les Prioux** about 150m after the bridge. Follow this path and cross the river at around 2045m. In spring the river crossing can be quite tricky, as the bridge over the stream has collapsed. Continue along the left bank of the stream to the Chalet des Nants (2184m). Follow the combe above the chalet to around 2300m then bear left (north-east) to reach the **Col des Thurges** (2679m). As some low cliffs bar access to the col itself, climb to the right (east) of the col so avoiding them. A short descent leads to the hut. (The tour can still be worthwhile late in the season when you have to carry your skis almost all the way to the hut). The winter 'room' of the hut is the middle of the three buildings.

The summer path offers a more direct way to the hut, avoiding the climb to the Col des Thurges. However, this path crosses some very steep slopes and can be dangerous if the snow is icy. As these slopes are also very avalanche-prone, the path should only be used if you are very sure of yourself and the snow conditions (or if there is no snow at all!)

Day 2: Traverse of the Dôme de Chasseforêt (3586m): The Refuge de la Valette (2554m) to the Refuge de l'Arpont (2309m)

Retrace your steps of the day before to the **Col des Thurges** (2679m). Continue due eastwards to reach the glacier at around 2900m. Follow this glacier (south-east) to below the **Dôme des Sonnailles** (3300m). Bear right

The climb is steep and sustained. A very early start is needed to have good conditions for the east-facing descent. Route finding for the final part of the descent to the hut can be tricky.

Starting Point:	Refuge de la Valette (2554m)
Finishing Point:	Refuge de l'Arpont (2309m)
Height Gain:	1030m
Time:	5 hours
Orientation:	South then east
Difficulty:	Quite difficult

(south) to reach the **Col de Chasseforêt** (3507m). A broad, low angled ridge leads to the summit.

Descend due east, to around 3100m, and then bear left slightly, to pass to the north of some cliffs. At 2900m, turn right (south-east) to reach the top of a wide south-facing slope, which leads directly to the hut.

It is also possible to descend due north from the summit and then head north-east to avoid an area of crevasses. At around 3300m, turn right (south-east) to join the above route at around 3100m.

Descending due south from the summit then turning left onto the **Glacier d'Arpont** at 3100m is a little less sustained, less direct and there are more crevasses.

Day 3: Traverse of the Col du Moine (3320m): The Refuge de l'Arpont (2309m) to the Refuge du Fond d'Aussois (2324m)

The Col du Moine is much less frequented than its northern neighbour, the Col du Labby, despite the fact that both its ascent and descent are more direct.

Starting Point:	Refuge de l'Arpont (2309m)
Finishing Point:	Refuge du Fond d'Aussois (2324m)
Height Gain:	1100m
Time:	5 hours
Orientation:	South-west
Difficulty:	Moderate

Climb due west to reach the **Glacier de l'Arpont** (2700m). Turn left and traverse almost horizontally southwards to reach the ridge (2780m) that separates the

Refuge du Fond d'Aussois

glacier from the **Ruisseau du Grand Pyx**. Make a descending traverse westwards to reach the base of this valley (2700m). Continue towards the west-south-west to reach the **Glacier de la Mahure** (2750m). Bear left (south) and follow the middle of the glacier to the col.

Descend due west across the **Glacier de Labby** to avoid some cliffs at 3000m. Contour round the western edge of the **Lac du Genepy** (2900m), staying above the lake, to cross the **Plan de la Gorma** (2800m). Bear right slightly to descend, more or less directly to the hut. Be careful not to go too far right as the terrain becomes quite complex and route finding is difficult.

The height for the Col du Moine that is marked on the map appears to be a misprint. Careful examination of the contours shows the col to be at about 3320m.

Day 4: Traverse of the Pointe de l'Observatoire (3015m): The Refuge du Fond d'Aussois (2324m) to the Refuge de Péclet-Polset (2470m)

From the hut head west towards the **Cime des Planettes** following a narrow gully through the rock bands about a kilometre from the hut (2450m). Steeper slopes lead

If you are sure of your ability, a more direct descent to the Refuge Péclet-Polset is possible via a steep gully between the Col d'Aussois and the Pointe de l'Obsevatoire. The view from the Pointe de l'Observatoire is exceptional. The Refuge Péclet-Polset has gas central heating!

Starting Point:	Refuge du Fond d'Aussois (2324m)
Finishing Point:	Refuge de Péclet-Polset (2470m)
Height Gain:	691m + 250m + 200m
Time:	6 hours
Orientation:	North then south
Difficulty:	Moderate

right (north) to a small col (2938m) just south of the Col d'Aussois. Traverse this first col then head east to the **Col d'Aussois** (2916m) and the steeper slopes which lead to the **Pointe de l'Observatoire** (3015m). The summit is reached by a very easy, 20m climb.

From the summit, descend to the **Col d'Aussois**. Turn left (north) and descend to the **Ruisseau de Rossoire** (2397m). Turn left and follow the streambed to reach a building at around 2200m. Put your skins back on your skis and climb due south below the rocks of the Pointe de Rossoire to reach an ill-defined ridge (2450m). From

Skinning up to the Col d'Aussois

the crest of the ridge, make a descending traverse, below the **Pointe de l'Observatoire**, to reach the bottom of the valley at around 2270m. Put your skins back on one more time for the final climb, due east, to the hut.

Day 5: The Dôme de Polset (3501m)

Starting Point:	Refuge de Péclet-Polset (2470m)
Finishing Point:	Les Prioux (1700m)
Height Gain:	1031m
Time:	5 hours
Orientation:	North then south-east then north
Difficulty:	Moderate

This is perhaps one of the most enjoyable tours that I have ever done. The skiing is very easy but the scenery absolutely magnificent.

Climb north-westwards from the hut to just above the **Lac Blanc** (2550m). Contour round the northern edge of the lake (the southern edge is more direct but the slopes

Approaching the Lac Blanc on the way up to the Dôme de Polset

on this side are much more avalanche prone) then climb south-east facing slopes towards the **Col du Souffre**. As soon as the angle eases (2750m), turn left (north) to follow the eastern branch of the **Glacier de Gebroulaz** to the summit.

From the summit, retrace your steps back to the hut. The final part of the descent along the Doron de Chavière Valley is obvious. Even late in the season you should be able to ski down to around 1900m.

ALTERNATIVES

DAY 1: Before the road to Les Prioux is open it is probably better to start the tour from the Refuge du Col de la Vanoise. A *randonneur* lift pass is available at Pralognan, allowing you to take the lifts to Les Barmettes. From the top of the lifts to the hut takes about 2hrs. After the Pont du Chanton, the way to the hut is marked by large posts. This does, however, make the descent from the Refuge de Péclet-Polset very long, especially if there is no snow for the last few kilometres.

DAY 2: The classic route from the Refuge du Col de la Vanoise to the Dôme de Chasseforêt is via the Col du Dard (3153m) and the Col du Pelve (2992m). Allow at least 4hrs for the climb, as there is a lot of distance to be covered.

From the Refuge de la Valette it is possible to do the traverse via the Dôme de Nants (3570m) or the Dôme de l'Arpont (3599m). The difficulty and time are about the same as for the Dôme de Chasseforêt.

DAY 3:   The traverse can be done via the Col de Labby rather than the Col du Moine. The difficulty and time are about the same.

If you want to miss out the Refuge du Fond d'Aussois, you can traverse the Passage de Rossoire (3479m, quite difficult), the Dôme de l'Arpont (3599m, quite difficult) or the Dôme des Nants (3570m, difficult) directly to the Doron de Chavière Valley.

DAY 4:   If you prefer to use guarded huts, the Refuge de la Dent Parachée (2520m) is a possible alternative to the Refuge du Fond d'Aussois, but it is not as well situated for the traverse of the Pointe de l'Observatoire.

One more day can be added to the circuit by traversing the Col de la Masse (2923m, moderate) to the Refuge de l'Orgère, perhaps taking in the Rateau d'Aussois (3131m, quite difficult) or the Grand Roc (3316m, difficult) on the way; The Refuge Péclet-Polset can be reached from the Refuge de l'Orgère via the Col de Chavière (2796m, moderate).

DAY 5:   If your legs are feeling tired the day can be shortened by stopping at the Col du Souffre (2819m, easy), the Col du Grand-Infernet (2841m, moderate) or the Col des Fonds (2907m, quite difficult). The Col de Chavière (2796m, moderate) is also a possible alternative.

CHAPTER EIGHT
Val d'Isère

INTRODUCTION

Before the advent of skiing as a sport for the masses, Val d'Isère was a very poor, run-down mountain village. The transformation into one of the most prestigious and expensive resorts in France has been quite spectacular. The reason for the resort's success is very simple however: the mountains on the south side of the upper Isère valley provide perfect skiing conditions. However, regulations have restricted development within the Vanoise National Park and, fortunately for ski tourers, the spread of the ski lifts has been contained. The happy result of this trade-off between development and conservation is very easy access to some wonderful wild skiing in areas where the presence of the resort is barely noticed.

This chapter describes two three-day tours that are

Skinning up to the Pointe de la Sana (Tour B, Day 3)

116

Tour Profile: Val d'Isère A and B Tours

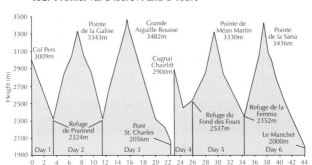

linked by their common start point – Val d'Isère. These are short tours but they can both be extended by incorporating some of the many possible variants described in the Alternatives section at the end of the chapter. When the resort is open, both of these tours are easily accessible using public transport; there is a regular bus service from the railway station in Bourg St. Maurice to Val d'isère.

The two tours are very different, although both should be within the capabilities of most competent skiers. The first tour visits the cirque at the head of the Isère river and describes two moderately difficult routes to the Pointe de la Galisse and the Grande Aiguille Rousse, which are accessible from the small and quite rustic Prariond hut. This cirque boasts almost a dozen possible ski touring objectives of all levels of difficulty. The two routes that I have described visit the highest skiable summits.

The second tour is a small circuit, to the south of Val d'Isère, which, despite the ease of access, has a very remote feel. Both the Pointe de Méan Martin and the Pointe de la Sana summits are great classics, with the latter being one of the most enjoyable easy ski tours in Savoie.

ACCESS

From Chambéry follow the A43 and A430 motorways or the N6 and N90 *routes nationales* to Albertville, and then continue along the N90 to Bourg St. Maurice. From Bourg St. Maurice follow the signs to Val d'Isère (D902). From Chambéry to Val d'Isère takes around an hour and forty-five minutes.

For the Refuge de Prariond, continue straight on, through the village, to Le Fornet. When the resort is open, this is the end of the road. however, from the beginning of May it is possible to drive up to the Pont St. Charles.

For the Refuge du Fond des Fours, park in the centre of the village. From the beginning of May, it is possible to drive up to Le Manchet.

Val d'Isère is easily accessible by public transport. There are regular train services to Bourg St. Maurice and a bus service from Bourg St. Maurice to Val d'Isère.

SNOW CONDITIONS

Good snow conditions can be found from January until June but the best time to go is usually mid-March to May. The area is much quieter at the end of the season and the avalanche risk, especially for the Grande Aiguille Rousse and the Pointe de la Sana, is much reduced by spring snow conditions.

MAPS

3633 ET Tignes, Val d'Isère

RESORT SKIING

The obvious choice is Val d'Isère. With 300km of pistes and numerous off-piste possibilities, the Espace Killy has enough to keep even the most demanding skier happy. If you want to get away from the big resort atmosphere of Val d'Isère, St.-Foy-Tarentaise has only 25km of pistes but vast areas of off-piste. It is also much cheaper than Val d'Isère!

TOUR A

Day 1: Val d'Isère (1950m) to the Refuge de Prariond (2324m)

Take the Fornet cable-car, then the **Vallon de l'Isèran gondola** and the **Cascade chairlift**. From the top of the chairlift, head north-north-east, past the **Montet draglift** and the **Grand Pisaillas chairlift**, to the **Col Pers** (3009m). From the col, descend more or less due north to the **River Isère**. Cross the river and head east-south-east to the hut.

Map Eight A: Val d'Isère Tour A

This is a classic off-piste descent, so you are unlikely to find virgin powder. During the spring, the snow on the descent is usually at its best between 11am and 2pm, depending on the weather and the exact time of year.

Starting Point:	Col Pers (3009m)
Finishing Point:	Refuge de Prariond (2324m)
Height Gain:	0m (from the top of the lifts)
Time:	30 minutes (from the top of the lifts)
Orientation:	North
Difficulty:	Easy

If you are allergic to ski lifts (or if the resort is closed), it is possible to climb directly to the hut by continuing along the road from the lifts to the **Pont St. Charles**. If there is a lot of snow you can follow the bottom of the Gorges du Malpasset but be careful, as this area is extremely avalanche prone. Later in the season it is usually necessary to follow the summer path along the northern edge of the gorge. From Le Fornet to the hut takes about 2hrs (about one hour from the Pont St. Charles).

Day 2: The Pointe de la Galisse (3343m)

Starting Point:	Refuge de Prariond (2324m)
Finishing Point:	Refuge de Prariond (2324m)
Height Gain:	1020m
Time:	5 hours
Orientation:	West then south
Difficulty:	Moderate

The first 250m of the descent is very easy, providing a nice warm-up for the more difficult middle section.

From the hut, head due north for a short distance, and then turn east-north-east to follow the **Ruisseau du Niolet** to a height of around 2650m. Turn left (north) to climb steeper slopes that lead up to and onto the **Glacier de Bassagne** (2900m). It is usually best to stay on the right bank of the glacier. At around 3100m, turn right (east) to follow gentler slopes to the summit. Descend by the same route.

Day 3: The Grande Aiguille Rousse (3482m)

Starting Point:	Refuge de Prariond (2324m)
Finishing Point:	Val d'Isère (1950m)
Height Gain:	1180m
Time:	5 hours
Orientation:	North
Difficulty:	Moderate (quite difficult if you ski direct from the summit)

As befits the highest summit in the area the views are magnificent. It is also possible to do an interesting circuit via the Col du Montet (see the Alternatives section at the end of the chapter).

Head due south from the hut to cross the river (2296m), and then climb sustained slopes to the west of the **Ruisseau du Gros Caval**. At around 2700m, make a gentle uphill traverse towards the south-east to pass under the north ridge of the **Pointe de Gros Caval** (2800m). Once past this ridge, gentler slopes lead towards the **Col du Montet**. At around 3150m, bear left to pass below the **Petite Aiguille Rousse** and arrive at a small col at 3368m (cornices possible). The summit ridge can be climbed on skis but it is much easier on foot. Descend to the col either by the same route or via the south face (steep and exposed). From the col, head north-north-west, across the **Glacier des Sources de l'Isère**. At the end of the glacier (2800m), bear left (north-west) to reach the **Ruisseau des Loses** (2450m). Turn left and head west-north-west to the hut. From the hut, head due west to reach the Gorges du Malpasset, and then the Pont St. Charles and Le Fornet.

ALTERNATIVES

DAY 1: Pointe Pers (3327m, quite difficult). From the Col Pers, descend to just above the Rocher du Léchoir (2800m). From here, climb steepening slopes south-south-eastwards to the summit.

Signal de l'Isèran (3237m, quite difficult). From the top of the Fornet cable-car, take the Signal draglift. From the top of the draglift, contour round to the east, to reach the foot of the Glacier du Grand Vallon. Climb the glacier, bearing south-west at around 3150m, to reach the summit. Descend back to the foot of the glacier, and then traverse right (east) to reach the Ruisseau du Léchoir and the hut.

DAY 2: Col de la Galise (2987m, easy), Col de la Vache (2955m, easy), Col d'Oin (3164m, easy): short, easy tours, ideal for newcomers to touring.

DAY 3: An excellent circuit can be done by descending the south face of the Grande Aiguille Rousse for 450m (slopes of up to 40° and quite exposed). At around 3000m, bear right to make a descending traverse into the combe, which leads to the Col du Montet. Climb to the col and follow the main itinerary back to the hut.

Grande Aiguille Rousse, north-east face (3482m, difficult). A good introduction to steep slopes and a great way to traverse this impressive summit, but access is sometimes made difficult by the formation of a cornice at the top.

Pointe du Gros Caval, (3285m, north-west face: moderate; east face: quite difficult)

TOUR B

Day 1: Val d'Isère (1840m) to
the Refuge du Fond des Fours (2537m)

The Cugnai bowl is another classic off-piste run. From Val d'Isère, take the Solaise Express chairlift, then a series of small chair- and draglifts, to reach the Cugnai chairlift. From the top of this lift, traverse into the Cugnai bowl and descend due west. At around 2600m, traverse

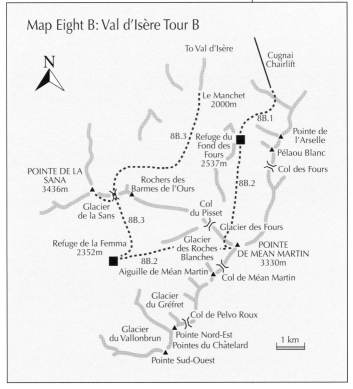

Map Eight B: Val d'Isère Tour B

N

To Val d'Isère

Cugnai
Chairlift

Le Manchet
2000m

8B.1

Pointe de
l'Arselle

8B.3   Refuge du
Fond des
Fours
2537m

Pélaou Blanc

Col des Fours

POINTE DE LA
SANA
3436m

Rochers des
Barmes de l'Ours

8B.2

Glacier
de la Sans

8B.3

Col
du Pisset

Glacier des Fours

Refuge de la Femma
2352m

Glacier
des Roches
Blanches

8B.2   Aiguille de Méan Martin

POINTE
DE MEAN MARTIN
3330m

Col de Méan Martin

Glacier
du Gréfret

Col de Pelvo Roux

Glacier
du Vallonbrun

Pointe Nord-Est
Pointes du Châtelard

1 km

Pointe Sud-Ouest

The Refuge du Fond des Fours is a superb little hut with a very friendly warden, but the warmth of the welcome can be more than offset by the chill of the dormitory, a separate building that can be extremely cold, even in the spring!

Starting Point:	Val d'Isère (1840m)
Finishing Point:	Refuge du Fond des Fours (2537m)
Height Gain:	100m (from the top of the lifts)
Time:	1 hour (from the top of the lifts)
Orientation:	North
Difficulty:	Easy

south-west to reach a point at an altitude of around 2450m. This is about mid-way between the Chalet des Fours and the hut. From this point it is a 30 minute climb, due south, to the hut. To reach the hut without using the lifts takes about 3hrs from Le Châtelard (when the resort is open) or about 2hrs from Le Manchet (from the beginning of May).

Day 2: Traverse of the Pointe de Méan Martin (3330m): The Refuge du Fond des Fours (2537m) to the Refuge de la Femma (2352m)

The Pointe de la Méan Martin is regarded as being a relatively safe itinerary but the avalanche risk should not be forgotten. If you are at all unsure of the stability of the snowpack take the longer, but safer route, via the Col du Pisset.

Starting Point:	Refuge du Fond des Fours (2537m)
Finishing Point:	Refuge de la Femma (2352m)
Height Gain:	800m
Time:	4 hours
Orientation:	North-west then west
Difficulty:	Moderate

From the hut, head due south to follow the **Ruisseau des Fours**. About 500m from the hut, turn right (south-west) to climb a short, steeper section that leads to the long plateau below the north face of the **Pointe de Méan Martin**. Continue due south to reach the **Glacier des Fours**, which is climbed on its right bank (quite steep for about 100m) to reach the north-west arête of the **Méan**

Descent from the Pointe de Méan Martin

Martin at around 3200m. Cross the arête and continue due south to climb the south face to the summit.

From the summit, descend the south face for about 100m, then turn right and descend due west onto the **Glacier des Roches Blanches**. At around 3000m, head north-west towards the **Ruisseau des Roches Blanches** (2850m). Follow the stream, heading west, to the hut. Cross over onto the northern side of the valley as soon as you can as the stream becomes difficult to traverse once you get lower than about 2450m.

One day in May I saw the debris of an enormous avalanche (500m across and at least a metre deep) that had scoured the entire north face of the Méan Martin and the Glacier des Fours the previous day.

Day 3: Traverse of the Pointe de la Sana (3436m): The Refuge de la Femma (2352m) to Val d'Isère (1840m)

From the hut, follow the **Ruisseau de la Femma**, first north-east, and then due north, until you get to a shallow **cirque** (2750m) headed by a line of cliffs. Follow a steep looking gully at the right-hand end of the cliffs to reach

The Refuge de la Femma, unfortunately, is typical of the new breed of mountain huts that have traded their rustic charm for creature conforts. Take a towel if you fancy a shower! The Pointe de la Sana is a magnificent, isolated summit with slopes at the perfect angle for enjoyable skiing: never too steep but quite sustained. This is, without a doubt, one of my favourite ski tours.

Starting Point:	Refuge de la Femma (2352m)
Finishing Point:	Val d'Isère (1840m)
Height Gain:	1080m
Time:	5 hours
Orientation:	South then north-west
Difficulty:	Moderate

a small, flatter area at around 2900m. Continue towards the north-west to reach the **Col des Barmes de l'Ours** (3077m). If you have heavy sacks, you can leave any unnecessary gear here and pick it up on the descent. From the col, sustained slopes to the west of the south-east arête lead directly to the summit. From the summit, descend to the Col des Barmes de l'Ours, and then head due north (a short, steeper section can be avoided on the left) to around 2900m. The easiest descent is to head due east from here, towards the **Lac des Pissets** (2600m), then north to reach the **Ruisseau du Pisset**, staying on the west bank of the stream. The stream can be followed

Skinning up to the Pointe de la Sana

The view to the south-east from the Pointe de la Sana

all the way back to Val d'Isère. The steeper slopes above the Saut du Pisset should be avoided unless you are sure that the snow-pack is stable.

ALTERNATIVES

DAY 1: The Pointe de l'Arselle (3110m, quite difficult), the Pélaou Blanc (3135m, quite difficult) and the Col des Fours (2976m, easy) are all easily accessible from the hut.

DAY2: The Col de Méan Martin (3103m, easy) is a shorter and easier alternative, as well as giving access to the traverse of the Aiguille de Méan Martin (3278m, quite difficult).

DAY 3: There are no real alternatives. Very good skiers can add an extra day or two to the tour by skiing the Col du Pelvo Roux (3219m, quite difficult) or the Pointes du Châtelard (3434m/3479m, difficult).

CHAPTER NINE
The Ambin Valley

INTRODUCTION

The Haute Maurienne Valley can be thought of, in many ways, as the 'land that time forgot'. The rush to create ski-resorts on every available mountainside was much less frenetic here than in the Tarentaise Valley, to the north. Though the modern world has had an impact, the Haute Maurienne has benefited from this more low-key development and now offers something very different to visitors – authenticity!

The Haute Maurienne stretches from Modane, in the west, to the Italian border, 60km to the east. The tours described fall within the three main ski-touring centres of this region: the Ambin Valley, the Avérole Valley and the area around the Carro and Evettes huts, all of which are on the southern and eastern edges of the area. The area to the north has been covered in the previous chapter.

The Ambin Valley is the most westerly of the Haute Maurienne areas described in this guide. It branches off

Tour Profile: Ambin Valley

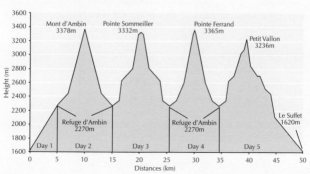

the main Maurienne Valley at Bramans (10km east of Modane) and runs east and then south for around 15km to the Col d'Ambin. Though it is the closest part of the Haute Maurienne to the main population centres of Chambéry and Grenoble, it is probably the least frequented of the valley's major ski-touring areas. That being said, the hut is quite small and is often full on public-holiday weekends. The warden is, however, very welcoming and does everything possible to make sure that you are comfortable and that the hut does not get over-crowded.

One of the wonderful aspects of the Ambin Valley is the feeling you get of being completely cut off from the rest of the world. This is excentuated by its long approach, especially at the beginning of the season, which leads to a haven of peace and beauty, far from the pressures of modern life. Even when the hut is full, the calm of the valley works its charm. The summits of the valley are not particularly high but they provide superb views of almost the entire chain of the French Alps from Mont Blanc to the Mercantour.

The head of the valley forms a north facing 'box' with four superb skiable summits at its corners. This is an ideal situation for what the French call a 'star tour', ie. several day trips branching out from one starting point. 'Star tours' have several advantages over traditional hut-to-hut tours. They allow you to explore one area more fully and, in many ways, they are more relaxing; you can get comfortably installed in one hut, your rucksack will be lighter and it is easier to shorten your itinerary in case of fatigue or bad weather. You do, however, lose the pleasure of having done a real journey through the mountains.

Despite having a common start point, the four tours described here have their own character and give different views and perspectives of this wildly beautiful valley. None are exceptionally difficult but they all involve 1000m or more of ascent; the cumulative fatigue over five days can be considerable. Shorter alternatives are described at the end of the chapter, together with a few steeper descents for more challenging skiing.

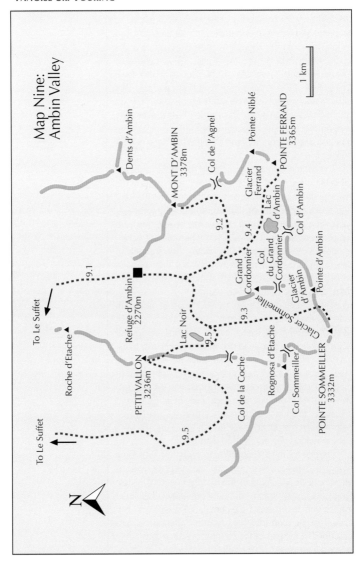

Map Nine:
Ambin Valley

1 km

Dents d'Ambin

Col de l'Agnel

MONT D'AMBIN
3378m

Pointe Niblé

POINTE FERRAND
3365m

Glacier
Ferrand

Lac
d'Ambin

Col d'Ambin

9.2

Grand
Cordonnier

Col
du Grand
Cordonnier

9.4

Pointe d'Ambin

To Le Suffet

9.1

Refuge d'Ambin
2270m

Glacier Sommeiller

Glacier
d'Ambin

9.3

Roche d'Etache

Lac Noir

9.5

PETIT VALLON
3236m

Col de la Coche

Rognosa d'Etache

Col Sommeiller

POINTE SOMMEILLER
3332m

To Le Suffet

9.5

N

ACCESS

From Chambéry, follow the A43 motorway or the N6 *route nationale* to Modane, and then follow the N6 to Bramans. At Bramans, turn off the main road and follow the D100 through the village to Le Suffet. Early in the season, the road is closed just outside Bramans, as the upper-part is used as a cross-country ski trail. There is a shuttle bus-service from outside the Bramans town hall (Mairie) to the start of the ski trail at Notre Dame de Déliverance. From Chambéry to Le Suffet takes about 1½hrs.

SNOW CONDITIONS

The best touring conditions are found from March to May, but the Ambin Valley has one of the longest ski seasons of any of the areas of the French Alps. In some years it is possible to ski from November until July! The Glacier Sommeiller was, at one time, considered a possible site for a summer ski-resort.

MAPS

3634 OT Val Cenis

RESORT SKIING

The nearest ski-resorts are Val Fréjus (52km of pistes), La Norma (65km of pistes) and Val Cenis (80km of pistes). All of these resorts have a good variety of skiing in a low-key family atmosphere. See Chapters 5 and 10 for ski tours that are accessible from these resorts.

Day 1: Le Suffet (1650m) to the Refuge d'Ambin (2270m)

From Le Suffet, follow the track along the left bank of the Ruisseau d'Ambin, crossing over to the right bank at the bridge at 1897m. When the track ends (1990m), follow the base of the valley due north for 2½km. The valley is then blocked by a small cliff, on top of which is the hut. Go around the eastern edge of the cliff to reach the hut.

The hut is unlikely to be overcrowded but Easter weekend can be very busy even if the road isn't open.

Starting Point:	Le Suffet (1650m)
Finishing Point:	Refuge d'Ambin (2270m)
Height Gain:	620m
Time:	2½ hours
Orientation:	North
Difficulty:	Easy

Up until at least the beginning of April, however, it is necessary to take a shuttle bus from Bramans to the Chapel of Notre Dame de Déliverance (1550m). The approach is then extremely long (around 12km, allow 4hrs).

Day 2: The Mont d'Ambin (3378m)

Follow the valley floor due north for about 1½km to where the stream divides (2330m). Continue due south,

Skinning up to the Refuge d'Ambin (Day 1)

Starting Point:	Refuge d'Ambin (2270m)
Finishing Point:	Refuge d'Ambin (2270m)
Height Gain:	1110m
Time:	6 hours
Orientation:	South then west then north
Difficulty:	Moderate

This is the highest summit in the area and an ideal vantage point from which to see the lie of the land. Be aware that the snow on the south facing slopes below the summit transforms very quickly.

passing a small cliff (which bars the way) on the left. At around 2500m, turn left (east) to climb steeper slopes towards the Col de l'Agnel (3091m). About 50m below the col, turn left again to climb sustained slopes to the summit. The last few metres along the south-east ridge are done on foot. Descend by the same route.

Day 3: The Pointe Sommeiller (3332m)

Starting Point:	Refuge d'Ambin (2270m)
Finishing Point:	Refuge d'Ambin (2270m)
Height Gain:	1060m
Time:	6 hours
Orientation:	East then north then east
Difficulty:	Moderate

The Pointe Sommeiller was once considered as a site for a summer ski area! Fortunately the project was abandoned but the area on the Italian side did suffer from the development of pylons and a road that almost reaches the Col Sommeiller. Recently the area has been cleaned up and the remaining scars of previous developments will soon be completely healed.

Follow the base of the valley (as Day 2) to where the stream divides. Turn right (north-west) to follow a shallow, south-east-facing gully to around 2600m. At the top of the gully, turn left (south) to make a gently ascending traverse towards the **Glacier Sommeiller**, passing the **Lacs Blancs** at around 2700m. Go past the **Grand Cordonnier**, bearing slightly south-eastwards, towards the **Pointe Ambin**. At around 3000m, the slope steepens markedly and leads to the ridge between the Pointe d'Ambin and the Pointe Sommeiller at around

3300m. Follow the ridge to the summit, the final section being done on foot. Descend by the same route.

Day 4: The Pointe Ferrand (3365m)

There are several ways to reach the summit of the Pointe Ferrand, all of which are of about the same difficulty. The route described here is the most direct.

Starting Point:	Refuge d'Ambin (2270m)
Finishing Point:	Refuge d'Ambin (2270m)
Height Gain:	1100m
Time:	6 hours
Orientation:	North-west
Difficulty:	Quite difficult

Follow the base of the valley (as Day 2) but continue following the streambed all the way to the **Lac d'Ambin** (2683m). Follow the northern shore of the lake to reach a well-defined, and quite steep, west-south-west facing gully, which leads to the **Glacier Ferrand**. Once on the glacier (3050m), head south-east to reach the foot of the summit ridge. If there is enough snow, the ridge can be skied all the way to the summit. Descend by the same route.

Day 5: Traverse of the Petit Vallon (3236m): The Refuge d'Ambin to Le Suffet

Follow your tracks from Day 3 to just past the **Lacs Blancs** (around 2700m). Follow a right curving arc, around a line of small cliffs, to reach the **Lac Noir** (2800m). From the lake, head north-west across steeper slopes to reach a small col (3085m) at the foot of the **Petit Vallon**. Traverse the col and climb the south-west face of the Petit Vallon, quite sustained, to reach a platform about 50m below the summit. Continue to the top on foot.

Starting Point:	Refuge d'Ambin (2270m)
Finishing Point:	Le Suffet (1650m)
Height Gain:	970m
Time:	6 hours
Orientation:	South then west then east
Difficulty:	Moderate

This is a superb traverse that allows you to visit another very wild valley. It is worth walking the final 50m to the summit, as the views are superb.

Descend the south-west face to around 2800m. Turn right and descend steeper, west facing slopes to a flat area at 2550m. Traverse north-westwards to reach the **Ruisseau du Côte Cornu** (2450m). Follow this stream (north-east) to reach the bottom of the **Vallée d'Etache** at 2108m. Follow the bottom of the valley then a track on the eastern side of the valley, back to **Le Suffet**.

Going up the Petit Vallon

ALTERNATIVES

DAY 2:   It is possible to descend the much steeper west face of the Mont d'Ambin (difficult, 600m at 35° or more). At around 2750m, head south to find a passage through the cliffs, which otherwise prevent a direct descent to the hut.

The Col de l'Agnel (3091m, moderate) provides a shorter alternative.

DAY 3:   The descent via the Glacier d'Ambin (quite difficult, 100m at just over 40°) provides a good introduction to skiing steeper slopes. This is a more interesting route at the end of the season as the valley below the Galcier d'Ambin holds the snow much longer than the east facing slopes below the Lacs Blancs.

The west-east traverse of the Col du Grand Cordonnier (2944m, moderate) is a short but quite spectacular tour. An early start is essential as the descent gets the sun very early.

Col Sommeiller (2993m, moderate).

DAY 4:   Pointe Niblé (3345m, moderate). A little shorter and a little easier at the end than the Pointe Ferrand.

The Col d'Ambin (2899m, moderate) via the Glacier d'Ambin is a nice little tour in its own right, but it also provides an interesting, although longer, approach to the Pointe Ferrand.

DAY 5:   A more direct descent can be done. Follow

the Ruisseau du Plan d'Etache from the foot of the south-west face of the Petit Vallon heading directly to the Vallée d'Etache. However, the exact line of the descent is difficult to see from above and its viability is very dependant on snow conditions.

The Col de la Coche (2947m, quite difficult) is the shortest route to the Vallée d'Etache but the final slopes below the col are steep.

OTHER ITINERARIES

There are many possibilities in the valleys to the west of the Ambin Valley, but most of them are very long and there are no huts. Unfortunately, the Refuge de la Bramanette is private and locked during the winter. The best way to explore this fabulous region is with a tent.

If you want to spend an extra day at the Refuge du Suffet, the Roche d'Etache (3083m, quite difficult, 600m at 30 to 35°) provides an excellent descent.

Skinning up to the Refuge d'Avérole with the Charbonnel in the background (Day 1)

CHAPTER TEN
Avérole

INTRODUCTION

The popularity of the Avérole Valley with ski tourers is demonstrated by the size of its hut. With 88 places it has the highest capacity of all the huts in the Maurienne Valley. (The Refuge de l'Arpont has 94 places in summer but only 24 are accessible during the ski-season). The short answer to the question 'Is this popularity justified?' is a quite resounding 'yes'. The Avérole Valley has been blessed with an extraordinary number of summits and cols that are easily accessible on skis.

The entrance to the valley is guarded by two very imposing summits, the Pointe de Charbonnel to the south and the Albaron to the north. The Charbonnel is a magnificent summit to do on skis but the climb is very long (almost 2000m) and a certain amount of luck is required to have good snow at the bottom and safe conditions higher up. Following the road up the valley, through the hamlet of Avérole, the eye is continuously drawn to the imposing north face of the Bessanèse, one

Tour Profile: Avérole

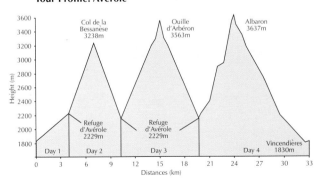

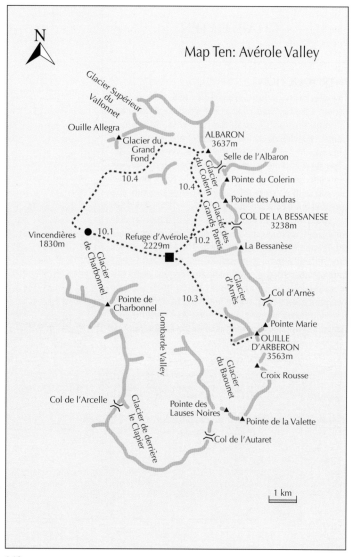

N

Map Ten: Avérole Valley

Glacier Supérieur du Vallonnet

Ouille Allegra

Glacier du Grand Fond

ALBARON
3637m

Selle de l'Albaron

Glacier du Colerin

Pointe du Colerin

10.4

10.4

Pointe des Audras

Glacier des Grands Pareis

COL DE LA BESSANESE
3238m

Vincendières
1830m

10.1

Glacier de Charbonnel

Refuge d'Avérole
2229m

10.2

La Bessanèse

Pointe de Charbonnel

10.3

Glacier d'Arnès

Col d'Arnès

Lombarde Valley

Pointe Marie

OUILLE D'ARBERON
3563m

Croix Rousse

Glacier du Baounet

Col de l'Arcelle

Glacier de derrière le Clapier

Pointe des Lauses Noires

Pointe de la Valette

Col de l'Autaret

1 km

of the few major summits that cannot be skied. Most of the other summits, however, are hidden in the twists and turns of the terrain above the Avérole Valley.

The Refuge d'Avérole is situated on a small knoll, just above the confluence of three valleys. These three valleys split again, higher up, to form a number of small combes. The largest of the three, the Lombarde Valley, continues south from the hut for 8km, finally ending at the Pointe du Fort. The first 5km of the valley are relatively flat, rising only 500m, making the approach to the summits at the head of the valley rather long and tedious. As this long approach puts off the vast majority of people, peace and quiet are guaranteed even at the busiest times of year.

The valleys to the south-east and north of the hut are much shorter and provide more interesting skiing. This chapter has three objectives: the Col de la Bessanèse as a relatively short but interesting introduction; the Ouille d'Arberon as one of the highest and best skiable summits to the south of the hut; the Albaron, which is quite simply an all time alpine ski-touring classic.

The best snow conditions are generally found at the end of the season, when the road is open as far as

Skinning up to the Refuge d'Avérole (Day 1) – the Bessanése in the background

Vincendières, but this is also a fantastic area to visit at the end of the winter, when the long approach from Bessans adds to the wilderness feeling.

ACCESS

From Chambéry, follow the A43 motorway or the N6 *route nationale* to Modane. Continue along the N6 to Lanslebourg, and then take the D902 to Bessans. Go through the village and park at the Bessannaise holiday centre. Bessans is approximately 1¼hrs from Chambéry. From mid-April onwards, the road is open as far as Vincendières, about 4km from the Bessannaise.

SNOW CONDITIONS

The touring season runs from March to the end of May, or even the middle of June in a good season. This area is often subject to easterly or south-easterly winds (The Lombarde) as well as the prevailing westerly and north-westerly winds associated with Atlantic depressions; wind-slabs can be a danger on almost any slopes, especially early in the season.

MAPS

3633 ET Tignes/Val d'Isère, 3634 OT Val Cenis

RESORT SKIING

The best resort skiing is to be found at Val Cenis. There are 70km of pistes, mostly blue and red. Val Cenis also gives access to some good tours, for example: The Pointe de la Ronce (3612m, quite difficult), the Pointe du Lamet (3504m, difficult, 150m at 45°), The Signal du Petit Mont Cenis (3162m, quite difficult, 500m at 35°) and The Pas de la Beccia (2717m, easy).

Bonneval has a few ski-lifts but the ski-area is much smaller than Val Cenis.

Bessans is a world-renowned cross-country ski area with 80km of trails.

Day 1: Bessans (1737m) to the Refuge d'Avérole (2229m)

Starting Point:	The Bessannaise holiday centre (1737m), 1km north of Bessans
Finishing Point:	Refuge d'Avérole (2229m)
Height Gain:	490m
Time:	3 hours
Orientation:	North-west
Difficulty:	Easy

At the beginning of the season, the long climb to the hut takes you along a road that is used as a Nordic ski trail. Beware of cross-country skiers descending as not all of them are in complete control of their skis!

Follow the road to **Vincendières** (1830m), either on skis or by car depending on the time of year. Continue along the road to Avérole (1990m) on foot (the road is closed to cars, except for residents, after Vincendières), from where an obvious track leads to the hut.

Day 2: The Col de la Bessanèse (3238m)

Starting Point:	Refuge d'Avérole (2229m)
Finishing Point:	Refuge d'Avérole (2229m)
Height Gain:	1010m
Time:	4 hours
Orientation:	West then south-west
Difficulty:	Moderate

This is quite a short tour but with superb, sustained skiing and magnificent views of the north face of the Bessanèse.

Head due north from the hut (a very short climb and descent) to reach the **Ruisseau du Veillet**. Follow the right bank of the stream to reach the northern end of the **Glacier des Grandes Pareis** (3000m). Turn right (east) and cross the glacier to reach the col. Descend by the same route.

Day 3: The Ouille d'Arbéron (3563m)

Starting Point:	Refuge d'Avérole (2229m)
Finishing Point:	Refuge d'Avérole (2229m)
Height Gain:	1340m
Time:	6 hours
Orientation:	West then north-west
Difficulty:	Quite difficult

Ouille is a local variation on the word *aiguille* meaning needle or pointed summit. The Ouille d'Arbéron is not really a needle but it is sharp enough to give breathtaking views of the wild valleys and summits surrounding it.

From the hut, a short descent (south-east) leads to the Ruisseau de l'Oney (2217m). Follow this narrow valley to where it widens out at around 2700m. Continue towards the south-east to reach the Col d'Arbéron (3022m). From the col, traverse across the Glacier d'Arbéron to reach the south-west ridge of the Ouille d'Arbéron at around 3200m. Follow the ridge to the summit. The last 150m are often too rocky to ski. Descend by the same route.

Day 4: Traverse of the Albaron (3637m)

Starting Point:	Refuge d'Avérole (2229m)
Finishing Point:	Vincendières (1830m) or Bessans (1737m)
Height Gain:	1420m
Time:	7 hours
Orientation:	West then south-west
Difficulty:	Quite difficult

The Albaron is THE classic summit of the area. The descent is varied, always interesting and very long. The view from the top is one of the best in Savoie.

Head due north from the hut (a very short climb and descent) to reach the Ruisseau du Veillet. Follow the right bank of the stream to an altitude of 2800m. Bear left (west) to traverse under a rocky ridge, then continue in the same direction to a height of around 2950m. Make a long traverse due north, losing as little height as possible, to reach the middle of the valley of the

Ruisseau d'Entre Deux Ris, at around 2900m. Continue due north to climb steepening slopes that lead to a small saddle at 3450m. Turn right (north-east) to reach the summit. The final slope is steep and rocky; getting to the summit generally involves a few metres of easy climbing.

From the summit, descend due west towards the Col du Grand Fond (3350m). Just before the col, turn left to follow the northern edge of the Glacier du Grand Fond, bearing left at around 3150m to head towards the Lac du Grand Fond (2876m). Do not go all the way to the lake, but at 2900m bear right (west) to go around the northern edge of a line of small cliffs. Be careful, these cliffs are not easy to make out from above. Once past the cliffs, follow the Ruisseau des Follièrses to Les Planars (2250m). Follow the track from Les Planars to the Avérole Valley. This track holds snow a surprisingly long time; it's often possible to ski all the way to the valley when the surrounding slopes are almost bare.

ALTERNATIVES

DAY 2: It is possible to descend into Italy and spend a night at the Alberto Gastaldi hut before coming back to Avérole via the Col d'Arnès. The eastern sides of both these cols are very steep.

Pointe des Audras (3244m, moderate)

DAY 3: Col d'Arnès (3012m, moderate)

Pointe Marie (3313m, quite difficult)

Croix Rousse (3571m, difficult, 400m at 35 to 40°) One of the best steeper slopes in the area.

Pointe des Lauses Noires (3384m, moderate) Very long but tranquillity guaranteed.

It would be impossible to list all of the alternatives that are available in this area, so I have just included the ones that are the most interesting.

DAY 4: It is possible to descend from the summit of the Albaron directly to Bonneval. The route finding is quite complex but this is perhaps a more interesting option at the end of the season than the south-facing descent to Vincendières. From the Col du Grand Fond, follow the northern branch of the Glacier Supérieur du Vallonnet to reach a passage through the cliffs at around 2650m. Head north-west to reach the Ruisseau du Vallonnet and then follow the pistes down to Bonneval.

Traverse to the Refuge des Evettes (see chapter eleven) via the Selle d'Albaron (3474m, quite difficult). The climb is steep but the descent is quite easy.

Pointe du Colerin (3475m, quite difficult). A little shorter than the Albaron, but also a little steeper. Descend back to the hut or directly to the hamlet of Avérole.

OTHER ITINERARIES

The Lombarde Valley has several possibilities, all of which are very long. One of the best is the traverse into the Ribon Valley via the Col de l'Arcelle (see Chapter 11). Beware of fragile snow bridges across the stream: a skier was killed in 2002 when a snow bridge collapsed.

Ouille Allegra (3130m, moderate). An interesting tour best done as a day trip from Bessans. By the time the road is open to Vincendières it is usually too late for this south-facing slope. The views are magnificent.

Pointe de Charbonnel (3752m, difficult). This is one of the most sustained descents in the Alps, with 1900m of descent at an average of over 30° and some short sections at up to 45°. Good conditions are rare as there needs to be stable conditions at the top yet enough snow in the bottom half to bank out some of the steeper, narrower sections. Even at the end of spring, massive slab avalanches can come down from the top section.

CHAPTER ELEVEN
Carro/Evettes

INTRODUCTION

This final chapter on the Haute Maurienne describes tours around the Refuge du Carro and the Refuge des Evettes. The area is best known for the Carro–Evettes–Avérole traverse which is one of the great classics of alpine ski touring (see the Alternatives section at the end of the chapter). The tour described here combines part of this traverse with some of the superb day trips that the area has to offer.

These two huts are very well positioned for short day trips and make the area ideal for ski tourers who would find 1000m of ascent every day a little too challenging. However, to ski all of the peaks directly from the summit requires a reasonable level of skiing ability, as the slopes are sometimes steep and exposed. (Less confident skiers can easily avoid the steepest sections of the descents.) A certain amount of mountaineering experience is also necessary as the glaciers that you cross, especially those to the south of the Col de Trièves and between the Pointe

Tour Profile: Carro/Evettes

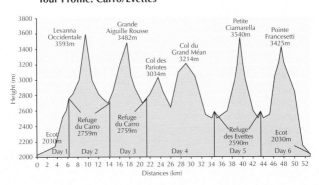

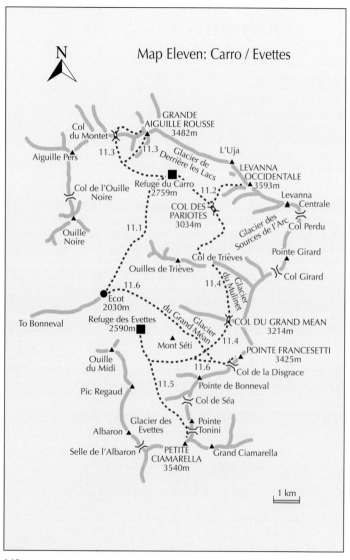

Tonini and the Albaron, are not entirely benign.

The Carro hut is a traditional stone building in a magnificent setting. The combe in which it is situated faces south and is quite open, giving magnificent views of the mountains to the south of the Arc Valley. The wardens are also extremely friendly and welcoming, making this all that a hut should be. The approach walk can be quite long, especially early in the season when the road is closed at Bonneval, so it is rare for the hut to be overcrowded. In marked contrast, the Evettes hut is a squat, modern, prefabricated building, but the spectacular surroundings of the Cirque des Evettes more than make-up for the shortcomings of the architecture. The approach to this hut is relatively short so it can be very busy at weekends.

ACCESS

From Chambéry, follow the A43 motorway or the N6 *route nationale* to Modane. Continue along the N6 to Lanslebourg and then take the D902 to Bonneval. Do not turn left into the village, but continue along the D902 to the first hairpin bend. Turn right here (opposite the Tourist

The final slopes below the Pointe Francesetti (Day 5) with the Grande Ciamarella and the Petite Ciamarella in the background

The approach to the Pointe Francesetti (Day 5)

Office) and then immediately right again, crossing the river. Park at the foot of the Vallonnet chairlift or, if the road is open, continue to Ecot. Bonneval is approximately 1¾hrs from Chambéry.

ESCAPE ROUTES

Refuge du Carro: descend directly back to the valley the same way that you went up.

   Refuge des Evettes: head south-west from the hut to the Col des Evettes. Turn right (north-west) to reach the Ruisseau du Picherse. Turn right again (north-east) to go around some rock bands before traversing back westwards to rejoin the Ruisseau du Picherse, which is followed to the valley.

SNOW CONDITIONS

The best touring conditions are found in April and May. At this time the snow-pack, which has had time to stabilise, is at its thickest and any crevasses are completely covered. The season can last from January until the middle of June, but spring snow conditions are generally necessary to ski many of the steeper slopes in reasonable safety (eg. Grande Aiguille Rousse, Petite Ciamarella). This is quite a windy area so the risk from wind-slab avalanches should never be underestimated.

MAPS

3633 ET Tignes, Val d'Isère

RESORT SKIING

The only downhill skiing to speak of is at Bonneval. There are 25km of pistes of all levels. A short ski tour, the Ouille du Midi (3042m, moderate) via the Glacier Inférieur du Vallonet, is easily accessible from the lifts. This is more than off-piste skiing as the glacier can have some quite big crevasses.

   The nearest ski-resort of any size is Val Cenis (16km from Bonneval), which has 80km of pistes of all levels.

   Bessans has one of the best cross-country ski areas in France.

The beginning of the climb to the Refuge du Carro, at the end of the season – the Grande Aiguille Rousse in the background.

Day 1: Ecot (2030m) to the Refuge du Carro (2760m)

Starting Point:	Ecot (2030m)
Finishing Point:	Refuge du Carro (2760m)
Height Gain:	730m
Time:	3 hours
Orientation:	South
Difficulty:	Easy

Walking to Ecot is not necessarily bad; the long walk puts many people off and thus the hut is less likely to be full.

Early in the season (up until the middle of April) it is usually necessary to park at Bonneval and walk along the road to Ecot. This adds 230m of ascent and a good hour to the approach. From the car park at **Ecot**, follow the track along the north side of the small reservoir. From here there are two possibilities depending on the snow conditions:

The Refuge du Carro

1) If there is sufficient snow, keep on the track until just before the hamlet of **La Duis** (2140m). Turn left (north) and follow the right bank of the **Ruisseau de Léchans** to a height of around 2450m. Bear left slightly to go around a small gorge. At around 2550m turn right (north-east) to cross a much flatter area. Steeper slopes then lead more or less directly to the hut.

2) Towards the end of the season it is better to branch off the main track at a height of 2118m and follow the line of the summer path, crossing a stream at around 2400m, before making a long rising traverse to join the previous route, just below the hut. Although this is less direct, the snow tends to last a lot longer here than on the slopes beside the Ruisseau de Léchans.

Skinning up to the Levanna Occidentale with the Grande Ciamarella in the background

Day 2: The Levanna Occidentale (3593m)

Starting Point:	Refuge du Carro (2760m)
Finishing Point:	Refuge du Carro (2760m)
Height Gain:	835m
Time:	5 hours
Orientation:	West then north-west
Difficulty:	Moderate

The Levanna Occidentale can be reached on skis but most people do the last 30m on foot. The view of the Gran Paradiso from the summit of the Levanna Occidentale is superb.

From the hut, head due east, descending slightly, to reach the **Lac Blanc** (2753m). Turn right (south-east) to reach a short, wide gully that is followed to slightly gentler slopes that lead to the **Col des Pariotes** (3034m). At a height of about 3000m bear left (due east) to the **Glacier de Derrière les Lacs** (this is quite undulating terrain: it is almost impossible to avoid one or two short descents). Follow the southern edge of the glacier to reach steeper, and often rocky, slopes that lead to the final arête at 3400m. Follow the south side of the arête to the summit. The descent is by the same route.

Day 3: The Grande Aiguille Rousse (3482m)

Starting Point:	Refuge du Carro (2760m)
Finishing Point:	Refuge du Carro (2760m)
Height Gain:	800m
Time:	5 hours
Orientation:	North then south
Difficulty:	Quite difficult

This route offers an excellent but intimidating descent; the steep top slopes are directly above a line of cliffs. If the snow is hard a fall could be very serious; reduce the risk by descending the final arête on foot, to the col at 3368m.

From the hut, head west along the line of the summer path, to an altitude of around 2700m (this is easier and faster without skins on your skis). Continue the traverse, moving slightly uphill, to a flat area at 2867m. From here, turn right (north-west) to reach the **Col du Montet** (3185m). The last 30m below the col are quite steep. From the Col du Montet, make a gently rising traverse eastwards to contour around the north-west ridge of the **Petite Aiguille Rousse**. After the ridge, turn south-eastwards and climb to a small col (3368m) situated between the Petite and the Grande Aiguille Rousse. From this col, follow the west ridge of the **Grande Aiguille Rousse** to the summit.

The descent follows the steep, south-facing slope directly below the summit (450m at an angle of up to 40°). However, the western side of this slope is a little gentler and less exposed. The exact line to take through the cliffs at the bottom of the slope depends on the snow conditions and should be examined during the climb. The end of the descent is much easier and follows the line of ascent back to the hut.

Day 4: The Carro–Evettes Traverse: The Col des Pariotes (3034m), the Col de Trièves (3100m) and the Col du Grand Méan (3214m)

This is part of what is recognised (even by Chamonix guides) as one of the great alpine ski-traverses. A brief description of a much longer version of this traverse is given in the Alternatives section at the end of this chapter.

Starting Point:	Refuge du Carro (2760m)
Finishing Point:	Refuge des Evettes (2590m)
Height Gain:	375m + 515m + 90m = 980m
Time:	6 hours
Orientation:	South then west
Difficulty:	Difficult

From the hut, head due east, descending slightly, to reach the **Lac Blanc** (2753m). Turn right (south-east) to follow a short, wide gully to slightly gentler slopes that lead to the **Col des Pariotes** (3034m). From the col

descend first south-west (to avoid some cliffs) then south-east. Once below the cliffs (2850m) contour around the head of the valley until directly below the eastern summit of **Ouilles de Trièves**: ideally you will not descend below about 2650m. Put the skins back on your skis and follow the steepening slopes south-eastwards, past the **Col de Trièves** (3000m), to reach the **Glacier du Mulinet** at a height of around 3100m. Continue due south to reach the **Col du Grand Méan** (3214m). From the col, make a gentle descent, again due south, across the **Glacier du Grand Méan** (the exact line depending on the state of the crevasses) to a position below the **Pointes de la Piatou**. Turn right (west) and descend to the **Plan des Evettes**. From the lake at 2539m, head north-north-west to reach the hut. The 90m climb to the hut is not always welcome at the end of the day!

Day 5: The Petite Ciamarella (3549m)

Descend due south from the hut (without skins!) to reach the **Plan des Evettes** (2502m). Cross the flat valley floor

This route offers the most difficult descent of the tour with a quite intimidating start. Furthermore, the glacier has many crevasses to watch for.

Starting Point:	Refuge des Evettes (2590m)
Finishing Point:	Refuge des Evettes (2590m)
Height Gain:	1050m
Time:	5 hours
Orientation:	North then north-west
Difficulty:	Difficult

and then climb gently, due south, to the **Glacier des Evettes** (2600m). When the glacier steepens, at around 2700m, bear slightly left to avoid an area of crevasses

Descending from the Pointe Francesetti with the Albaron in the background

and seracs. A flatter section, at 2850m, leads directly towards the **Petite Ciamarella**. At around 3000m, bear left (due east) to climb gradually steepening slopes to the **Col Tonini** (3244m). Just before the col, turn right to climb steep, north-facing slopes to the summit. The last few metres are generally done on foot. The descent is by the same route.

Day 6: The Pointe Francesetti (3425m)

Starting Point:	Refuge des Evettes (2590m)
Finishing Point:	Ecot (2030m)
Height Gain:	920m
Time:	5 hours
Orientation:	North-west
Difficulty:	Moderate

Descend due south from the hut (without skins!) to reach the **Plan des Evettes** (2502m). Cross the flat valley floor, to the lake in the middle of the Plan des Evettes (2539m). Put the skins on your skis and climb west-facing slopes below the **Pointe de Bonneval**. At around 3050m, turn left (north) to avoid an area of crevasses, and then turn right (east) to follow gentle slopes to the **Col de la Disgrace** (3225m). At the col turn left (north) to climb steeper slopes (not as steep as they first appear) to the summit. Many people do this last part in crampons but, given reasonable snow conditions, it is not too difficult on skis.

For the descent, retrace your steps to around 3050m then head north-west to follow the **Ruisseau du Grand Méan**, passing to the north of the **Mont Séti**, back to **Ecot**. The exact line of descent will depend on snow conditions, but is usually best to stay on the right bank of the Ruisseau du Grand Méan as long as possible.

The Pointe Francesetti is, deservedly, one of the most popular ski-tours in the Haute-Maurienne. However, the lower slopes of the descent can be quite avalanche-prone, especially at the beginning of spring, as the snow rests on very smooth rock slabs. If you have any doubts about the stability of these lower slopes, it is better to descend via the hut (Col des Evettes) and the Ruisseau de Picherse.

ALTERNATIVES

DAY 1: The Refuge du Carro can be reached from Val d'Isère via the Col de l'Ouille Noire (3229m, easy). If you use this access route, it is logical to combine the tours around the Refuge du Carro with those around the Refuge de Prariond (see Chapter 8).

DAY 2: The Uja (3379m, easy) provides a shorter and easier day.

DAY 3: The Grande Aiguille Rousse can be traversed by climbing the Pas du Bouquetin (3335m), gaining the summit via the north-east arête. This is a much shorter trip (in terms of distance) but, as the slopes are very steep, it requires very stable snow conditions and a certain amount of mountaineering experience.

DAY 4: There are several excellent tours to do on the Glacier des Sources de l'Arc, especially if you are not continuing to the Refuge des Evettes. The most popular are the Col Perdu (easy, 3285m), the Col Girard (3050m, easy) and the Pointe Girard (3259m, moderate). These tours are also accessible as day trips if you are staying in Bessans or Bonneval.

DAY 5: Pointe Tonini (3327m, moderate). This is a shorter and easier day which offers magnificent views.

The Albaron (3637m, quite difficult) via the Selle de l'Albaron (3474m) and the south-east ridge. Although not really difficult this tour does require a certain amount of mountaineering experience. It is perhaps more interesting as a means of access to the Refuge d'Avérole than as a round trip.

DAY 6: There are no real alternatives.

OTHER ITINERARIES

The Grand Traverse: If you are prepared to accept the logistics involved (public transport from Albertville to Val d'Isère, taxi and public transport from the Ribon Valley back to Albertville), it is possible to do a magnificent five-day traverse from Val d'Isère to Bessans via the Prariond, Carro, Evettes and Avérole huts, finishing in the Ribon valley to the west of the Pointe de Charbonnel.

The much shorter Carro – Evettes – Avérole traverse is recognised as one of the best ski trips in the Alps and (if you don't have two cars) only involves a short taxi ride from the finishing point (Bessans or Vincendières) back to the start point at Ecot.

CHAPTER TWELVE
Ski Mountaineering

INTRODUCTION

This final chapter is different to the previous eleven in that it describes four individual summits that cannot easily be combined with a multi-day tour, either because of their difficulty or because of their isolation. The Grande Casse (3852m), the Aiguille des Glaciers (3816m), Mont Pourri (3779m) and the Aiguille de la Grande Sassière (3747m) are four of the five highest mountains in Savoie (the top five would include the Pointe de Charbonnel (3752m), see Chapter 10). They are described from north to south, starting with the Aiguille des Glaciers. All of these tours require a certain amount of mountaineering experience (or should be done with a mountain guide). For Mont Pourri and the Grande Casse, an excellent level of skiing ability is also necessary.

Skinning up to the Refuge du Col de la Vanoise (Grande Casse, Day 1).with the Aiguille de la Grande Glière (on the left) and the Aiguille de la Vanoise (on the right) in the background

The Aiguille des Glaciers (3816m)

The Aiguille des Glaciers is the most northerly summit to be described in this guide, and the only one to lie within the Mont Blanc massif. Although access from the Mont Blanc side is possible via the Glacier de Tré la Tête, the route is quite long and difficult. Access from the south is much easier, the only (minor) problem being the late opening of the access road. It is also from the south that the Aiguille des Glaciers is seen at its best – a proud sentinel guarding the route to Mont Blanc.

Paradoxically, this is both the easiest ski descent in this chapter and the most difficult summit to reach. Most people only go as far as the top of the Glacier des Glaciers at 3700m. The final section to the summit involves a 120m ice or mixed climb (depending on the conditions) of around AD/D standard. The ski descent is very sustained but never very steep: the Aiguille des Glaciers would make an ideal introduction to high-mountain ski touring. The best period in which to tackle this route is between May and early June – the period is limited by the opening of the road. Accommodation can be found at the Refuge Robert Blanc (2750m). This is an excellent little privately owned hut.

Whether you climb to the top, or whether you stay at the highest skiable point, the views of the Dômes de Miage, the Aiguille de Bionnassay and the south face of Mont Blanc are breathtaking.

ACCESS

From Chambéry, follow the A43 and A430 motorways or the N6 and N90 *routes nationales* to Albertville. From Albertville, continue along the N90 to Bourg St. Maurice. In Bourg St. Maurice, turn left onto the D902, which leads to the Cormet de Roseland and Les Chappieux. This road is usually opened at the beginning of the second week in May. After about 14km, turn right towards Les Chappieux. Go through the village and continue along the road to the Ville des Glaciers. The

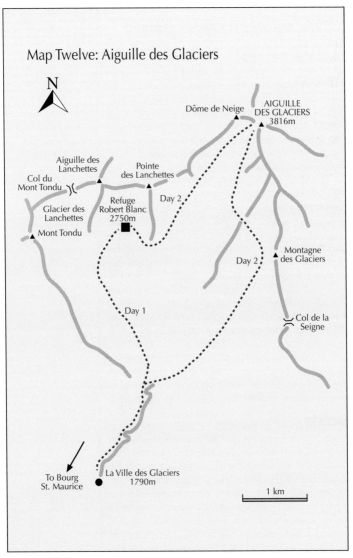

Map Twelve: Aiguille des Glaciers

N

Dôme de Neige

AIGUILLE
DES GLACIERS
3816m

Aiguille des
Lanchettes

Pointe
des Lanchettes

Col du
Mont Tondu

Day 2

Glacier des
Lanchettes

Refuge
Robert Blanc
2750m

Mont Tondu

Montagne
des Glaciers

Day 2

Day 1

Col de la
Seigne

To Bourg
St. Maurice

La Ville des Glaciers
1790m

1 km

road now becomes a dirt track: it is often possible to continue as far as the first hairpin bends at around 1850m. To get to the Ville des Glaciers from Chambéry takes almost 2hrs.

ITINERARY

Starting Point:	Ville des Glaciers (1790m)
Finishing Point:	Ville des Glaciers (1790m)
Height Gain:	960m + 1140m = 2100m
Time:	3hrs + 6hrs = 9hrs
Orientation:	South
Difficulty:	Quite difficult

Although the descent is not difficult, there are some very big crevasses: choose your line of descent with care!

Day 1: Follow the track from the **Ville des Glaciers** (1790m) to the **Chalet des Lanchettes** (1960m). Continue due north, to reach the **Ruissseau des Lanchettes**. Follow the stream (north-north-west) to an altitude of around 2400m. Bear right (north-east) to work your way through some rocky slopes that bar entry to the Combe Noire. Continue north-eastwards to the hut.

Day 2: Descend south-eastwards from the hut to go around the south ridge of the **Pointe des Lanchettes** at around 2560m. Put your skins on your skis and climb north-eastwards to reach the foot of the **Glacier des Glaciers** (2750m). Continue in the same direction, staying on the western edge of the glacier. Just below the **Dôme de Neige** (3550m), turn right (east) to reach the top of the glacier at around 3700m. There are several snow/ice gullies which lead to the summit, all of which are of similar difficulty. The choice depends on the quality and quantity of snow. The standard route is via the central gully (45° to 50° ice). The west face, to the left of the central gully, may provide an easier alternative, especially now that several bolts have been placed to protect the most difficult sections. Both of these routes are of *Assez Difficile* to *Difficile* standard.

The descent from the top of the glacier follows the eastern side of the **Glacier des Glaciers**, below the **Petite Aiguille des Glaciers**. Descend due south to around 3100m. From here there are two choices depending on snow conditions. If there is enough snow, it is possible to continue due south, staying just to the west of **Les Cabottes**, to reach the floor of the valley at around 1950m. If there is less snow, turn left (east) at around 3050m to cross the ridge above Les Cabottes and traverse into a snow bowl to the east of Les Cabottes. Descend south-eastwards to around 2800m, and then bear right (south) to go under the **Montagne des Glaciers**. At around 2650m, bear right again (south-west) to follow the **Ruisseau des Cabottes** back to the **Vallée des Glaciers**.

The Aiguille de la Grande Sassière (3747m)

The usual way of climbing the Aiguille de la Grande Sassière, both in winter and in summer, is from the south via Le Saut; the alternative from Le Chenal is too long for most people to do in one day (more than 2100m of height gain) and there is no hut. For skiers this means undertaking a traverse from Le Saut to Le Chenal, as the best descent is via the Glacier de la Sassière and the Nant Cruet Valley. There is however another possibility, one rarely considered for ski trips in the Alps, and that is

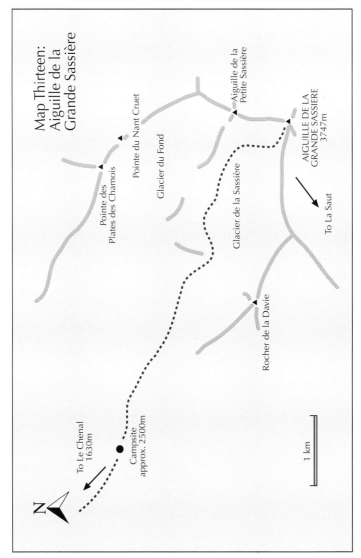

Map Thirteen: Aiguille de la Grande Sassière

Pointe des Plates des Chamois

Pointe du Nant Cruet

Glacier du Fond

Aiguille de la Petite Sassière

AIGUILLE DE LA GRANDE SASSIERE 3747m

Glacier de la Sassière

To La Saut

Rocher de la Davie

To Le Chenal 1630m

Campsite approx. 2500m

N

1 km

camping along the way. Camping in the Nant Cruet Valley, allows you to split the climb into two more reasonable legs and to truly savour the wild atmosphere of this magnificent valley. I have suggested camping at around 2500m, but there are lower campsites, at around 2100m, if you prefer not to carry the tent so far. The best time to undertake this route is between April and June.

This route for the Aiguille de la Grande Sassière is one of the wildest and most beautiful ski tours in the region, despite being only a stone's throw from Tignes.

ACCESS

From Chambéry, follow the A43 and A430 motorways or the N6 and N90 *routes nationales* to Albertville. From Albertville, continue along the N90 to Bourg St. Maurice. In Bourg St. Maurice, follow signs for the D902 to Tignes/Val d'Isère. About 22km from Bourg St. Maurice, just before the first avalanche tunnel at Les Pigettes, turn left onto the minor road to Le Chenal. To get to Le Chenal from Chambéry takes almost 2hrs.

ITINERARY

The central part of the glacier has a lot of crevasses. The final slope below the summit is often very icy.

Starting Point:	Le Chenal (1630m)
Finishing Point:	Le Chenal (1630m)
Height Gain:	870m + 1250m = 2120m
Time:	3hrs + 7hrs = 10hrs
Orientation:	North-west
Difficulty:	Difficult, 200m at 40° to 45° (if you ski from the summit, otherwise: quite difficult)

Day 1: Follow the track from **Le Chenal**, south, to the hamlet of **Nantcruet**. Bear left (south-east) to reach the **Nant Cruet Valley** at around 2100m; here there are some possible campsites you

may consider staying on. Otherwise, follow the valley to a flat area at around 2500m and camp here.

Day 2: From the campsite, head east-south-east to climb steep slopes to the right of a line of cliffs, bearing left (east) at around 2750m to reach the glacier at 2800m. Continue due east to below the **Aiguille de la Petite Sassière** (3300m). Turn right (south) and make an ascending traverse to reach the west ridge of the **Grande Sassière** at around 3500m. Follow the ridge to the summit. This is generally done on foot as it is steep and quite exposed.

If you do not intend to ski from the summit, you can leave your skis at the foot of the final ridge.

The steep triangular slope below the summit can be descended directly to around 3500m. From here follow the ascent route back to **Le Chenal**.

The Mont Pourri (3779m)

At first sight, there would seem to be only one possible way of descending Mont Pourri on skis. Though this is more or less true, the difficulty comes from trying to decide which approach to use to appreciate the mountain at its best. All of the routes descend via the Glacier du Geay, but there are at least three ways of reaching the summit. The traditional way is a two-day trip from the Peissey-Nancroix Valley, spending the night at the Refuge du Mont Pourri. The most difficult way, but the most complete from a mountaineering point of view, is to do a three-day circuit of the massif, taking in the Dôme des Platières, the Dôme de la Sache and finishing by the Mont Pourri. This circuit uses the Mont Pourri and the Turia huts. However, the simplest way, starting from Les Arcs, is described here on the assumption that the majority of visiting skiers are likely to come when the resort is open (up until the end of April). The best time to do this tour is April to June.

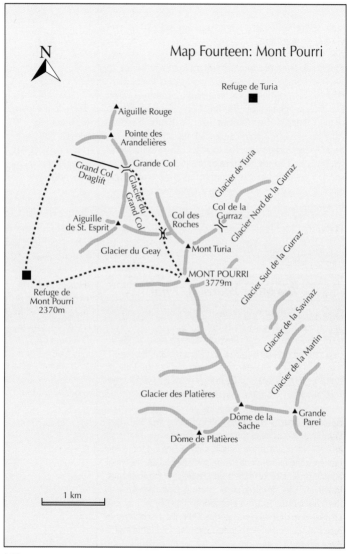

N

Map Fourteen: Mont Pourri

Refuge de Turia

Aiguille Rouge

Pointe des
Arandelières

Grande Col

Grand Col
Draglift

Glacier de Turia

Glacier Nord de la Gurraz

Col de la
Gurraz

Col des
Roches

Aiguille
de St. Esprit

Glacier du Grand Col

Mont Turia

Glacier du Geay

MONT POURRI
3779m

Glacier Sud de la Gurraz

Refuge de
Mont Pourri
2370m

Glacier de la Savinaz

Glacier de la Martin

Glacier des Platières

Dôme de la
Sache

Grande
Parei

Dôme de Platières

1 km

When the resort is closed it is better to spend the night at the Refuge du Mont Pourri and do a round trip via the Glacier du Geay. The hut can be reached from Arc 2000, via the Lac des Moutons, or from the Chalet de Rosuel in the Peissey-Nancroix valley.

ACCESS

From Chambéry, follow the A43 and A430 motorways or the N6 and N90 *routes nationales* to Albertville. From Albertville, continue along the N90 to Bourg St. Maurice. In Bourg St. Maurice, turn right onto the D119, which you follow to Arc 2000. If you are intending to spend a few days at Les Arcs, it is better to leave your car in Bourg St. Maurice and take the funicular railway to the resort.

ITINERARY

Starting Point:	Arc 2000, top of the Grand Col draglift (2935m)
Finishing Point:	Arc 2000, top of the Grand Col draglift (2935m)
Height Gain:	810m + 380m + 200m = 1390m
Time:	7 hours
Orientation:	North-west then south-west
Difficulty:	Difficult (several slopes at 40°, 50m at 45° near the summit)

It is important to be on the first lift in the morning and to move quickly if you want to have good conditions for the descent. Both the Glacier du Grand Col and the Glacier du Geay are quite heavily crevassed.

From the **Grand Col** (2935m), follow the left bank of the **Glacier du Grand Col** (due south), traversing leftwards at around 3300m to reach the **Col des Roches** (3443m). The last 200m below the col are steep and sustained. The col is not the most easterly depression in the ridge, nor the lowest. A 40m descent, on foot (in-situ cables), leads to the **Glacier du Geay**. Head south across the glacier, crossing the bergschrund at 3500m (not always easy) to reach the west ridge of **Mont Pourri**. Follow the ridge to the summit. The last 50m are at 45° and often icy.

Descend by the ascent route to below the **Col des Roches**. Continue down the right bank of the glacier (crevasses) below the **Aiguille de St. Esprit**. At around 2850m, turn left to follow south-west facing slopes to the **Refuge du Mont Pourri** (2380m). A 200m climb, due north, leads to the **Lac des Moutons** and **Les Arcs**.

The Grande Casse (3852m)

The Grande Casse is the highest mountain in Savoie and a must for all ski mountaineers. As befits the highest point for almost 50km, the views are sensational; on a clear day you can see most of the major summits of the southern Alps, the Mont Blanc massif and many of the giants of the Swiss and Italian Alps. The descent is also second to none: the added bonus of 100m of easier skiing at the beginning of the descent acts as a warm-up to the steep and sustained central section. The Grande Casse will delight all experienced skiers but good technique is essential; a fall could be extremely serious. Fortunately, due to the sunny aspect of the descent, good spring snow conditions occur quite frequently, making both the climb (generally on foot for the steeper sections) and the descent a little easier. The best time to attempt this route is from April to the beginning of June.

The Refuge du Col de la Vanoise (2517m) is, perhaps, the one negative aspect of this tour. It is not a particularly aesthetically pleasing building and, although it is enormous (152 places when it is guarded), it does get very busy being at the centre of a very popular ski touring area. Booking is essential.

ACCESS

From Chambéry, take the A43 and A430 motorways or the N6 and N90 *routes nationales* to Albertville. Follow the N90 to Moutiers. In Moutiers, take the D915 to Bozel, then to Pralognan-la-Vanoise. When the resort is open, buy a randonneur ski-pass to take the lifts to the Refuge des Barmettes (2010m). When the resort is closed you can drive up to Les Fontanettes (1644m).

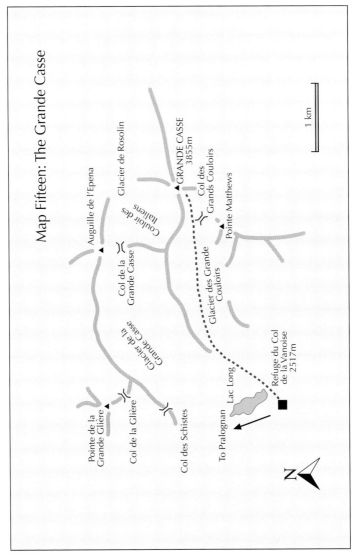

Map Fifteen: The Grande Casse

1 km

GRANDE CASSE
3855m

Glacier de Rosolin

Auguille de l'Epena

Col des
Grands Couloirs

Coloir des
Italiens

Pointe Matthews

Col de la
Grande Casse

Glacier des Grande
Couloirs

Glacier de la
Grande Casse

Refuge du Col
de la Vanoise
2517m

Lac Long

Pointe de la
Grande Glière

Col de la Glière

Col des Schistes

To Pralognan

N

ITINERARY

Even the steepest parts of the Glacier des Grands Couloirs have been climbed on skis, but most people will feel more comfortable with crampons and an ice-axe.

Starting Point:	Les Fontanettes (1644m)
Finishing Point:	Les Fontanettes (1644m)
Height Gain:	970m + 1380 = 2350m
Time:	3hrs + 6hrs = 9hrs
Orientation:	West
Difficulty:	Very difficult (400m at 40° to 45°)

Day 1: Follow the pistes north-east from **Les Fontanettes** to the **Refuge des Barmettes** (2010m). Cross the stream behind the hut and follow the track to the **Lac des Vaches** (2318m). Continue due east, close underneath the Aiguille de la Vanoise, until above the **Lac Long**. Turn right and head south to the hut.

Day 2: From the hut, descend to the **Lac Long** (2467m), and then follow south-west facing slopes to reach the foot of the **Glacier des Grands Couloirs** at around 2750m. Follow the right bank of the glacier, which steepens at around 3300m, to the **Col des Grands Couloirs** (3700m). Turn left (north-east) at the col and climb to the base of the west ridge of the **Grande Casse** (3750m). The ridge is followed, usually on foot, to the summit.

Descend by the same route to around 2600m. Go around the northern end of the **Lac Long** to reach the **Lac des Vaches** and then **Les Fontanettes**.

GLOSSARY

Avalanche probe	A thin, 2.5 to 3m-long metal pole that is used to localise an avalanche victim
Bergschrund	The gap that forms, between the ice and the mountain, at the head of a glacier.
Cornice	An accumulation of snow on the crest of a ridge or at a summit. Cornices can form quite large and fragile overhangs. You should never go too close to the edge of a ridge or summit without being certain of what is under your feet.
Couteaux/harscheisen	Metal crampons that can be attached to skis to improve their grip on hard snow.
Crevasse	A fissure in the surface of a glacier. In winter, all but the largest crevasses are buried under a layer of snow, but there is often enough snow to form solid snow-bridges. Linear depressions on the surface of a glacier may warn of the presence of a crevasse.
Département	A territorial division for local administration, similar to an English county.
Duvet	A jacket with an insulating layer of duck/goose down or synthetic fibres.
Gîte d'étape	Hostel type accommodation, similar to a mountain hut but close to a road.
Gîte rural/gîte de france	A holiday cottage.
GPS	Geographical Positioning System. A navigational aid using satellite data.

Ice-screws	Solid or tubular metal bars, used to provide anchor points in ice.
Jumars	A mechanical device used for climbing up a rope.
Mountain hut	Basic hostel style accommodation in the mountains.
Nevé	Hard packed snow that has been consolidated by freeze-thaw action.
Prussick loops	Loops of thin climbing rope that can be used for climbing up another rope. Several forms of non-slip knot can be tied.
Refuge	See Mountain hut.
Ripple marks	Small wave marks on the surface of the snow formed by the action of the wind. They are analogous to the marks sometimes seen in the sand at the beach.
Serac	An ice cliff that forms at the nose of a glacier or when there is a significant change of slope. Seracs are very dangerous as the downhill motion of the glacier can cause the cliff to collapse at any moment. Serac falls are totally unpredictable: never linger under a serac!
Skin	A self-adhesive layer of hair that is attached to the base of skis for climbing. The hair is arranged so that the ski can slide forwards but not backwards. They were originally made from seal-skins (hence the name) but are now either synthetic or made from mohair.
Snow dunes	Accumulations of snow, analogous to sand dunes.

Snow shovel

A lightweight, foldable shovel that can be used for digging an avalanche victim out of the snow.

Spring snow

Snow that has been compacted and consolidated by a period of freeze thaw. The snow is very hard in the morning, becoming very wet and slushy in the afternoon. When only the top centimetre or two has melted it provides one of the most enjoyable and easiest surfaces to ski on.

Touring skis

Touring skis are generally lighter than standard downhill skis and are fitted with special bindings with an articulated toe piece. For the climb, the binding is used with the heel free, as for a cross-country ski. The heel is locked for the descent, as for a standard downhill ski.

Transceiver

An electronic beacon for localising an avalanche victim. In transmission mode, the transceiver emits a signal that can be detected by other transceivers once they have been switched to reception mode. These devices enable a skier, who has been buried under an avalanche, to be found much more quickly. However, to use them efficiently requires a certain amount of practice. Fatal cases of interference between avalanche transceivers and mobile phones have been documented.

APPENDIX 1
Mountain Hut List

Most of the huts used by the tours in this guide are run by the French Alpine Club or by the Vanoise National Park. Both of these organisations have websites, which give some information about their huts. Visit the French Alpine Club: at www.clubalpin.com and the Vanoise National Park at www.vanoise.com. The others are either private or run by the local council.

The information given in the table was correct at the beginning of June 2002. The dates when huts are guarded vary slightly from year-to-year, depending on the dates of the French school holidays. The facilities provided by huts can also change, especially for huts that are not guarded. Where marked N/A the accommodation is more 'hotel style', so the question of using a sleeping bag or cooking for yourself does not arise.

Abbreviations: Y = yes   N = no   N/A = not applicable   O/R = on request

Name	Tel. No. Hut/Warden	Dates Guarded	Places: Guarded/ Not Guarded	Blankets	Stoves	Utensils
LAUZIERE						
Relais du lac Noir	04 79 36 30 52	All year	N/A	N/A	N/A	N/A
BELLEDONNE						
L'Oule	04 76 97 53 67	Not Guarded	20	Y	N	N

La Petite Valloire	04 76 45 18 21	Not Guarded	10	N	N	N
Merlet	04 76 97 53 67	Not Guarded	8	N	N	N
BEAUFORTAIN						
La Coire	04 79 09 70 92/ 06 82 12 40 42	Not Guarded	40	Y	Y	Y
Presset	04 79 33 05 52	Not Guarded	22	Y	Y	Y
La Balme	04 79 09 70 62	Not Guarded	30	Y	Y	Y
VALLOIRE						
Aiguilles d'Arves	04 79 59 01 77/ 04 79 20 41 39	March to May	54/15	Y	Y	Y
MONT THABOR						
3-Alpini	00 39 122 902 071	Weekends only	40/0	N/A	N/A	N/A
I Re Magi	00 39 122 964 51	Weekends + O/R	40/0	N/A	N/A	N/A
Ricou	04 92 21 17 04	On request	19/0	N/A	N/A	N/A
Drayères	04 92 21 36 01/ 04 92 21 37 28	March to May + O/R	64/40	Y	Y	Y
Mont Thabor	04 79 20 32 13	March to May O/R	46/38	Y	Y	Y
NORTH VANOISE						
Plaisance	No telephone number	Not Guarded	46	Y	Y	Y
La Glière	04 79 55 02 64	Not Guarded	12	Y	Y	Y

Name	Tel. No. Hut/Warden	Dates Guarded	Places: Guarded/ Not Guarded	Blankets	Stoves	Utensils
GLACIERS DE LA VANOISE						
La Valette	04 79 22 96 38/ 04 79 08 71 36	Not Guarded	44	Y	Y	Y
L'Arpont	04 79 20 51 51/ 04 79 20 54 32	Not Guarded	28	Y	Y	Y
Fond d'Aussois	04 79 20 39 83	Not Guarded	28	Y	Y	N
Péclet-Polset	04 79 08 72 13/ 06 63 68 46 92	30/03 to 28/04	78/18	Y	Y	Y
La Dent Parachée	04 79 20 32 87/ 04 79 20 36 81	15/03 to 12/05	36/30	Y	Y	Y
VAL D'ISERE						
Prariond	04 79 06 06 02/ 04 79 07 21 31	30/03 to 09/05	42/16	Y	Y	Y
Fond des Fours	04 79 06 16 90/ 06 87 13 41 24	28/03 to 08/05	44/24	Y	Y	Y
La Femma	04 79 05 45 40/ 04 79 20 33 00	30/03 to 09/05 + O/R	68/24	Y	Y	Y

	Phone	Guarded	Beds			
AMBIN VALLEY						
Ambin	04 79 20 35 00/ 04 79 20 34 60	April to May	30/30	Y	Y	Y
Suffet	04 79 05 30 17/ 04 79 05 04 46	O/R	40/0	Y	N/A	N/A
AVEROLE VALLEY						
Averole	04 79 05 96 70/ 04 79 05 81 33	16/03 to 12/05 + O/R	88/25	Y	Y	Y
CARRO/EVETTES						
Carro	04 79 05 95 79/ 04 79 37 51 64	16/03 to 05/05 + O/R	72/24	Y	Y	Y
Evettes	04 79 05 96 64/ 06 87 83 90 62	16/03 to 19/05 + weekends O/R	78/18	Y	Y	Y
AIGUILLE DES GLACIERS						
Robert Blanc	04 79 07 24 22	May/June	45	Y	Y	Y
MONT POURRI						
Mont Pourri	04 79 07 90 43/ 06 11 10 02 05	Weekends O/R	50/50	Y	Y	Y
Turia	04 79 62 30 54	Not Guarded	20	Y	Y	Y
GRANDE CASSE						
Col de la Vanoise	04 79 08 25 23/ 04 79 08 70 60	23/03 to 12/05 + weekends O/R	150/28	Y	Y	Y

APPENDIX 2
Tourist Information Offices

Information about accommodation, public transport, taxis and guides offices can be obtained from local Tourist Information offices. The information they give about weather and snow conditions is, however, usually very general and of little use in planning a tour. French Tourist Offices usually only have information about their own commune, but they will be able to direct you to the correct office if they cannot help you themselves.

LAUZIERE

Moutiers: tel. 04 79 24 04 23   www.ot-moutiers.com

Valmorel: tel. 04 79 09 85 55   www.valmorel.com

Aiguebelle: tel. 04 79 36 29 24

La Chambre: tel. 04 79 56 33 58

St. François-Longchamp: tel. 04 79 59 10 56

BELLEDONNE

Allevard: tel. 04 76 45 10 11
                                         www.allevard-les-bains.com

St. Colomban-
des-Villards: tel.04 79 56 24 53

BEAUFORTAIN

Aime: tel. 04 79 55 67 00

Beaufort: tel. 04 79 38 38 62

VALLOIRE

Valloire: tel. 04 79 59 03 96   www.valloire.net

Valmeinier: tel. 04 79 59 53 69   www.valmeinier.com

MONT THABOR

Valféjus/Modane: tel. 04 79 05 33 83   www.valfrejus.com

Névache   tel. 04 92 21 38 19

VANOISE NORTH

Champagny-en-Vanoise   tel. 04 79 55 06 55   www.champagny.com

Bozel: tel. 04 79 55 03 77   www.bozel.com

La Plagne: tel. 04 79 09 02 01   www.la-plagne.com

VANOISE GLACIER/GRANDE CASSE

Pralognan-la-Vanoise: tel. 04 79 08 79 08   www.pralognan.com

VAL D'ISERE/GRANDE SASSIERE

Val d'Isère: tel. 04 79 06 06 60   www.valdisere.com

Tignes: tel. 04 79 40 04 40   www.tignes.net

AMBIN VALLEY

Bramans: tel. 04 79 05 03 45

Aussois: tel. 04 79 20 30 80   www.aussois.com

AVEROLE VALLEY

Bessans: tel. 04 79 05 96 52   www.bessans.com

CARRO/EVETTES

Bonneval-sur-Arc: tel. 04 79 05 95 95 www.bonneval-sur-arc.com

AIGUILLE DES GLACIERS

Bourg St. Maurice: tel. 04 79 07 04 92 www.bourgstmaurice.com

MONT POURRI

Peisey-Vallandry: tel. 04 79 07 94 28 www.peisey-vallandry.com

Les Arcs: tel. 04 79 07 12 57 www.lesarcs.com

INFORMATION CAN ALSO BE OBTAINED FROM:

Agence Touristique
de la Savoie: tel. 04 79 85 12 45 www.savoie-tourisme.com

The Agence Touristique produces accommodation guides for the whole of Savoie.
The guide *Gîtes d'étapes et Refuges* by Annick and Serge Mouraret is updated and published annually by Rando Editions. It is updated every year.

For train schedules: www.sncf.com

For bus schedules: www.transavoie-modane.com
www.transavoie-moutiers.com

NOTES

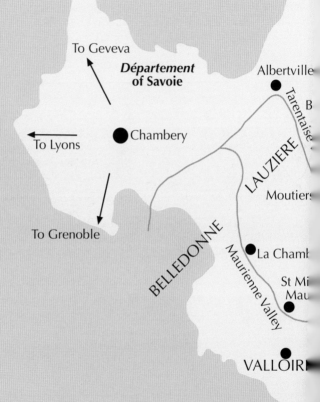

N

To Geveva

Département of Savoie

Albertville

Tarentaise

B

Chambery

To Lyons

LAUZIERE

Moutiers

To Grenoble

BELLEDONNE

La Chamb

Maurienne Valley

St Mi
Mau

VALLOIR

THE VANOISE AND SURROUNDING AREA

ITALY

Aiguille des Glaciers
3816m

BEAUFORTAIN   Bourg St. Maurice

River Isère   Mont Pourri
3779m

se Valley

Aiguille de la Grande Sassière
3747m

Grande Casse
3852m

VAL D'ISERE

CARRO / EVETTES

Bonneval

GLACIERS DE LA VANOISE

ore

River Arc

AVEROLE

chel de urienne

Modane

AMBIN VALLEY

ITALY

MONT THABOR

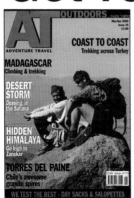

LISTING OF CICERONE GUIDES

- BORDER PUBS & INNS -
  A WALKERS' GUIDE
- CAIRNGORMS, WINTER CLIMBS
  5TH EDITION
- CENTRAL HIGHLANDS
  6 LONG DISTANCE WALKS
- WALKING THE GALLOWAY HILLS
- WALKING IN THE HEBRIDES
- NORTH TO THE CAPE
- THE ISLAND OF RHUM
- THE ISLE OF SKYE A WALKER'S
  GUIDE
- WALKS IN THE LAMMERMUIRS
- WALKING IN THE LOWTHER HILLS
- THE SCOTTISH GLENS SERIES
  - 1 - CAIRNGORM GLENS
  - 2 - ATHOLL GLENS
  - 3 - GLENS OF RANNOCH
  - 4 - GLENS OF TROSSACH
  - 5 - GLENS OF ARGYLL
  - 6 - THE GREAT GLEN
  - 7 - THE ANGUS GLENS
  - 8 - KNOYDART TO MORVERN
  - 9 - THE GLENS OF ROSS-SHIRE
- SCOTTISH RAILWAY WALKS
- SCRAMBLES IN LOCHABER
- SCRAMBLES IN SKYE
- SKI TOURING IN SCOTLAND
- THE SPEYSIDE WAY
- TORRIDON - A WALKER'S GUIDE
- WALKS FROM THE WEST HIGHLAND
  RAILWAY
- THE WEST HIGHLAND WAY
- WINTER CLIMBS NEVIS & GLENCOE

IRELAND
- IRISH COASTAL WALKS
- THE IRISH COAST TO COAST
- THE MOUNTAINS OF IRELAND

WALKING AND TREKKING IN THE ALPS
- WALKING IN THE ALPS
- 100 HUT WALKS IN THE ALPS
- CHAMONIX TO ZERMATT
- GRAND TOUR OF MONTE ROSA
  VOL. 1 AND VOL. 2
- TOUR OF MONT BLANC

FRANCE, BELGIUM AND LUXEMBOURG
- WALKING IN THE ARDENNES
- ROCK CLIMBS BELGIUM & LUX.
- THE BRITTANY COASTAL PATH
- CHAMONIX - MONT BLANC
  WALKING GUIDE
- WALKING IN THE CEVENNES
- CORSICAN HIGH LEVEL ROUTE:
  GR20
- THE ECRINS NATIONAL PARK
- WALKING THE FRENCH ALPS: GR5
- WALKING THE FRENCH GORGES
- FRENCH ROCK
- WALKING IN THE HAUTE SAVOIE
- WALKING IN THE LANGUEDOC
- TOUR OF THE OISANS: GR54
- WALKING IN PROVENCE
- THE PYRENEAN TRAIL: GR10
- THE TOUR OF THE QUEYRAS

- ROBERT LOUIS STEVENSON TRAIL
- WALKING IN TARENTAISE &
  BEAUFORTAIN ALPS
- ROCK CLIMBS IN THE VERDON
- TOUR OF THE VANOISE
- WALKS IN VOLCANO COUNTRY

FRANCE/SPAIN
- ROCK CLIMBS IN THE PYRENEES
- WALKS & CLIMBS IN THE PYRENEES
- THE WAY OF ST JAMES
  LE PUY TO SANTIAGO - WALKER'S
- THE WAY OF ST JAMES
  LE PUY TO SANTIAGO - CYCLIST'S

SPAIN AND PORTUGAL
- WALKING IN THE ALGARVE
- ANDALUSIAN ROCK CLIMBS
- BIRDWATCHING IN MALLORCA
- COSTA BLANCA ROCK
- COSTA BLANCA WALKS VOL 1
- COSTA BLANCA WALKS VOL 2
- WALKING IN MALLORCA
- ROCK CLIMBS IN MAJORCA, IBIZA &
  TENERIFE
- WALKING IN MADEIRA
- THE MOUNTAINS OF CENTRAL
  SPAIN
- THE SPANISH PYRENEES GR11
  2ND EDITION
- WALKING IN THE SIERRA NEVADA
- WALKS & CLIMBS IN THE PICOS DE
  EUROPA
- VIA DE LA PLATA

SWITZERLAND
- ALPINE PASS ROUTE, SWITZERLAND
- THE BERNESE ALPS A WALKING
  GUIDE
- CENTRAL SWITZERLAND
- THE JURA: HIGH ROUTE & SKI
  TRAVERSES
- WALKING IN TICINO, SWITZERLAND
- THE VALAIS, SWITZERLAND -
  A WALKING GUIDE

GERMANY, AUSTRIA AND EASTERN EUROPE
- MOUNTAIN WALKING IN AUSTRIA
- WALKING IN THE BAVARIAN ALPS
- WALKING IN THE BLACK FOREST
- THE DANUBE CYCLE WAY
- GERMANY'S ROMANTIC ROAD
- WALKING IN THE HARZ
  MOUNTAINS
- KING LUDWIG WAY
- KLETTERSTEIG NORTHERN
  LIMESTONE ALPS
- WALKING THE RIVER RHINE TRAIL
- THE MOUNTAINS OF ROMANIA
- WALKING IN THE SALZKAMMERGUT
- HUT-TO-HUT IN THE STUBAI ALPS
- THE HIGH TATRAS

SCANDANAVIA
- WALKING IN NORWAY
- ST OLAV'S WAY

ITALY AND SLOVENIA
- ALTA VIA - HIGH LEVEL WALKS
  DOLOMITES
- CENTRAL APENNINES OF ITALY
- WALKING CENTRAL ITALIAN ALPS
- WALKING IN THE DOLOMITES
- SHORTER WALKS IN THE
  DOLOMITES
- WALKING ITALY'S GRAN PARADISO
- LONG DISTANCE WALKS IN ITALY'S
  GRAN PARADISO
- ITALIAN ROCK
- WALKS IN THE JULIAN ALPS
- WALKING IN SICILY
- WALKING IN TUSCANY
- VIA FERRATA SCRAMBLES IN THE
  DOLOMITES

OTHER MEDITERRANEAN COUNTRIES
- THE ATLAS MOUNTAINS
- WALKING IN CYPRUS
- CRETE - THE WHITE MOUNTAINS
- THE MOUNTAINS OF GREECE
- JORDAN - WALKS, TREKS, CAVES ETC.
- THE MOUNTAINS OF TURKEY
- TREKS & CLIMBS WADI RUM
  JORDAN
- CLIMBS & TREKS IN THE ALA DAG
- WALKING IN PALESTINE

HIMALAYA
- ADVENTURE TREKS IN NEPAL
- ANNAPURNA - A TREKKER'S GUIDE
- EVEREST - A TREKKERS' GUIDE
- GARHWAL & KUMAON -
  A TREKKER'S GUIDE
- KANGCHENJUNGA -
  A TREKKER'S GUIDE
- LANGTANG, GOSAINKUND &
  HELAMBU TREKKERS GUIDE
- MANASLU - A TREKKER'S GUIDE

OTHER COUNTRIES
- MOUNTAIN WALKING IN AFRICA -
  KENYA
- OZ ROCK - AUSTRALIAN CRAGS
- WALKING IN BRITISH COLUMBIA
- TREKKING IN THE CAUCASUS
- GRAND CANYON & AMERICAN
  SOUTH WEST
- ROCK CLIMBS IN HONG KONG
- ADVENTURE TREKS WEST NORTH
  AMERICA
- CLASSIC TRAMPS IN NEW ZEALAND

TECHNIQUES AND EDUCATION
- SNOW & ICE TECHNIQUES
- ROPE TECHNIQUES
- THE BOOK OF THE BIVVY
- THE HILLWALKER'S MANUAL
- THE TREKKER'S HANDBOOK
- THE ADVENTURE ALTERNATIVE
- BEYOND ADVENTURE
- FAR HORIZONS - ADVENTURE
  TRAVEL FOR ALL
- MOUNTAIN WEATHER

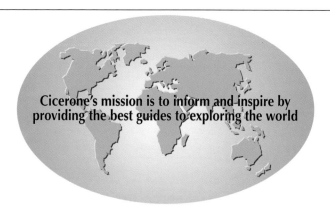

Cicerone's mission is to inform and inspire by providing the best guides to exploring the world

Since its foundation over 30 years ago, Cicerone has specialised in publishing guidebooks and has built a reputation for quality and reliability. It now publishes nearly 300 guides to the major destinations for outdoor enthusiasts, including Europe, UK and the rest of the world.

Written by leading and committed specialists, Cicerone guides are recognised as the most authoritative. They are full of information, maps and illustrations so that the user can plan and complete a successful and safe trip or expedition – be it a long face climb, a walk over Lakeland fells, an alpine traverse, a Himalayan trek or a ramble in the countryside.

With a thorough introduction to assist planning, clear diagrams, maps and colour photographs to illustrate the terrain and route, and accurate and detailed text, Cicerone guides are designed for ease of use and access to the information.

If the facts on the ground change, or there is any aspect of a guide that you think we can improve, we are always delighted to hear from you.

Cicerone Press
2 Police Square Milnthorpe Cumbria LA7 7PY
Tel:01539 562 069   Fax:01539 563 417
e-mail:info@cicerone.co.uk   web:www.cicerone.co.uk

CICERONE